MEANDERING
AROUND ENGLAND
in a Motorhome

Thomas Lewin

Grosvenor House
Publishing Limited

This book is published by
Grosvenor House Publishing Ltd
Link House
140 The Broadway, Tolworth, Surrey, KT6 7HT.
www.grosvenorhousepublishing.co.uk

A CIP record for this book
is available from the British Library

ISBN 978-1-80381-581-7

AUTHOR'S NOTE

The reader will often notice I refer to me and us, us and our. Well, I apologise. I realised at the time, or shortly afterwards, that I was referring to my wife, Bet, when she wasn't with me on that particular journey. I considered correcting it afterwards but then thought, why should I? Because in simple truth, even when she wasn't with me in person, she was with me in spirit, and she still is. When I am travelling around the Dales, walking along the seafront in Barmouth, Weymouth, up in the Pyrenees mountains, Lake Matemole, or on the beach in Gruissan on the Riviera, Bet is with me. You cannot eliminate 45 years of marriage.

Most people who get married only spend a few hours around or with each other during the week or the year until retirement if the marriage lasts that long. During our marriage, we were together 24 hours a day, 7 days a week, 52 weeks a year. Whether it was running a transport business, a country pub or shop or a hotel, she was with me, or rather, we were together.

To my beautiful, modest, shy wife, Bet, know I always loved you. I just never realised how much. One day, let us dance around the world.

To my lovely grandkids, Bobbie, Mitchel, and Sammy. You were delightful company that gave me a great deal of pleasure. Thanks for accompanying me on some of our little jaunts.

Just remember, and remember it well, make the most of your life, and don't waste it all on the working treadmill of life only to end up with nothing but the state pension eking your last days out. I've seen it far too many times. Have a great life.

FOREWORD

I've read and enjoyed most of Tommy Lewin's life stories, from his first outing as an author with Against the Odds - the story of humble family roots and his battle with dodgy cops in the Slums of Birmingham's Summer Lane - and his rise to prosperity and business success in The Climb Up and Away. His breakaway publishing venture, Touring Europe on a Budget, revealed more of a man with natural intelligence, enviable energy and curiosity - plus some tips on trimming the cost of seeing the world. All are tales which will appeal to Sun readers, many of whom are having to keep spending under control as the cost-of-living bites. Each of them has seen Tommy grow as a storyteller. Now his latest, and his best: Meandering Around England in a Motorhome. More and more are choosing to staycation in the UK. A quarter of a million families are driving campervans which offer freedom and home comforts at an affordable price. Another great read, Tommy.

Trevor Kavanagh – *Editor, The Sun*

MEANDERING AROUND ENGLAND IN A MOTORHOME

Let's be clear from day one if you've bought a camper with the idea of enjoying happy days tootling around England, stopping off at will in romantic, maybe isolated little spots in the many hundreds of beautiful places spread throughout the country, think again because you ain't welcome.

It's a sad fact of English life that many councils don't want us on their turf unless it's on the turf they dictate; a campsite. These are usually dotted around outside of the main towns or resorts where you can be managed, kept out of sight except to show your face and spend your hard-earned money before disappearing back to your little grassy pitch. Nice enough in the summer to sit outside, awning, chairs and barby out, birds singing. Not so much fun when it's belting it down with rain. The pitch is muddy, and it's a few hundred yards to the toilets and shower blocks. For that, you are charged a right few quid and expected to be grateful.

Years ago, in the good old days, campsites were the place to go to with your caravan or tent. If you were adventurous, you might find the odd farmer willing to rent you his field for a couple of quid, a bargain for you and a much-needed few quid for him. For the caravanner, the campsite was ideal, cheap, with the toilet block and tipping facilities nearby. For the tenter, a place to pitch up, fill the need to live 'au naturel', cook a few baked beans and bacon on the little Calor gas stove, sit cross-legged singing

'Home on the Range'. A place you could take your girlfriend without having the indignity of digging a hole to do your business. A field was for the lads, mates mucking in together. For the girlfriend, it was the campsite where you could go to a proper toilet in a quickly knocked up concrete block, a standpipe in the field for fresh water for your little camping kettle.

With a knapsack on your back, you could venture out into the wild, exploring the fields, hills, streams and rivers. Returning to a little campfire, a little fry up, and a lumpy bed on the grass in a nice warm sleeping bag, cuddled up with the love of your life.

For the caravanner, it was different, having set up your little home on wheels, awning out, table and chairs set with a bottle of wine, a simple meal cooked on the indoor four-ring gas cooker where you could sit in your nice casual clothes looking smugly over at the campers in the tent in next pitch. After a meal, you could hop into your car and drive out to explore the local amenities.

All this for just a couple of quid a night, nicely affordable for a couple of nights or a week, leaving you with a bit of spending money. No one was greedy, and each party was happy to have a few quid extra. That was then. Today it's a different ball game. Now the motorhome started poking its little two-litre engine into the scene. First, it was just the little Volkswagen camper, tight as it was with its raised roof and two beds and a little built-in cooker; it opened the door for the more adventurous. With the camper, you could drive to anywhere you wanted, exploring far and wide, parking up anywhere that took your fancy, in a field, on a beach, free, freedom at its best, far better than the alternative, a hotel or a little guest house that took your money kicked you out after breakfast, locked the doors and didn't let you back in till dinner.

Today it's changed out of all proportion (except for the guest houses, of course). Camping organisations have shot up and jumped on the bandwagon, the caravan and camping club, and caravan and motorhome club, each one with the umbrella to catch all or as many as they can. Each is welcome at each venue, except if your motorhome is too big, then you're told quite clearly you ain't welcome. The pitches are clearly marked out. Today, the pound signs have lit up the farmers' eyes.

The caravan and camping clubs are charity-run, meaning no one is making a profit. Whilst the prices are top bat, more than a lot of privately owned sites, you don't mind. In fact, they have become more popular because they don't make a profit. I wish I'd got into this charity game years ago, big salaries at the top, cheap labour at the bottom on the door taking your money, some working for very little or the privilege of a free pitch for the season, and people are queuing up for the privilege. Well, it's a charity, ain't it? We're not being ripped off because no one is making a profit. All our money goes to charity, and they roll the profits over year after year into more sites, making even more money. It's never-ending, and no one questions the fortune you're paying for a grass pitch in a field and slightly better toilet blocks. It's all set up for you, the camper. What a shrewd move.

Many people join the caravan and camping clubs because of the CLs. These are small sites shipped out to small farmers or country pubs with an allowance of five pitches only. The benefit of these to the farmer or smallholder is it gives him an extra few quid to put in his pocket, to the publican a bit of extra pocket money whilst gaining a few extra customers, some hope. Running a pub, you quickly find out that campers don't want to use your pub or pay for food and drinks when they have it all on tap, so to speak, with their own food and booze.

I speak from experience, having bought a country pub in Hereford with five acres and a small well-set-out CL. Great, until the first ones turned up and came over with the first six quid, for that they were using all our facilities and sucking three quid a night in electric. The little wheel in our meter was going around like a spinning top. Worse, no one was coming in to spend in the bar or restaurant. Meanwhile, the camping clubs were charging twenty-five quid a night plus. No, no, no, we soon put a stop to that matey, except for the most desperate or unconcerned owners of CLs, who would soon pull out.

Coincidentally, as the caravan and motorhome owners increased, so did the prices of the sites. This also coincided with the realisation by the local councils that the growing motorhome fraternity was not spending money in the local community. The site owners also, over the years, have found out how to ramp up the price even higher, so you might be quoted £30 for a pitch. Hmmm, ok, except that's just for the pitch. Then there is extra for each person or child over two.

If you have five kids and three dogs, you're in big trouble, plus the extra quid to use the shower. Then you have another couple of quid to put your awning out, then another couple of quid per dog, and before you know it, the price has shot up to 40 quid. Oh no, that's not included in the price, don't be silly.

Over the years, this has just crept up slowly, insidiously, without many of us realising, 'well, I'm only going for three nights; it's not a lot'. Together with a fortnight once a year, 'well, it's not a lot. We can afford it.' You were almost made to feel like a cheapskate if you pulled a face and complained. Now it's almost cheaper to drive to a hotel car park and book in for your holiday break. Sometimes, it is cheaper. It becomes a very unnecessary and expensive hobby for us and many others with a motorhome and the time and inclination to enjoy our leisure time.

My wife, Bet, and I had toyed with many ideas to enjoy our increasing leisure time as our retirement drew closer. A villa or apartment in Spain or the Canaries, perhaps. We tried it in Los Americana's, maybe a nice static in the country or by some nice seaside resort. Quite appealing till you look into it and realise you're paying a small fortune in ground rent. Besides, the caravan you've paid for not only deteriorates in value but you're also offered a pittance for it by the site owner to whom you must give the first option. If you sell it privately, the site owner takes a chunk of that. We'd heard some right horror stories, and you can't do anything about it because it's all legal.

We tried a caravan. All that towing? What about a folding caravan? It would fit in the garage when not in use, but then it's back to the towing again. How about a big six-berth tent that folds into the boot, and we can afford nice blow-up beds, all the comforts? Well, we tried that; it took half the day to put the thing up and hours to dismantle it, and even then, we lost bits and pieces, which we only noticed on our next outing. No. Then we saw the motorhome.

FINDING THE RIGHT MOTORHOME

For no particular reason other than a nice day out, we visited the camping and caravanning exhibition at the NEC, Birmingham. We'd sold our pub in 2005 (a terrible and stupid mistake on my part, i.e. buying it in the first place) and were looking at different options when we visited.

Anyone who has been to the NEC will know how big it is. It has million-pound boats, down to car toppers, and little pop-up tents that sit on top of the car. No, we couldn't see ourselves doing that. There were tents of all shapes and sizes and different alternatives. After a decent walk around with plenty of refreshments in between, we came to the motorhomes, not having even considered a motorhome. They took away our breath with what was on show. Small campers and big juggernauts with every facility you could think of.

The first one we came to was the Benimar, a Spanish-made motorhome that struck us as amazing, all posh and roomy. It even had a fixed bed and a garage underneath at the rear. A garage! Ideal for a scooter/moped as well as all the paraphernalia like tables and chairs, even air conditioning. Very impressive indeed, all for thirty grand. We were half sold on the idea, but first to have a good look around.

Our next port of call, the stand next door, was the Hymer stand. The only size that stood out to us was the mid-size model circa 21—22ft. Walking in to look around, I wasn't very impressed at all. Dull looking as we looked around inside, I couldn't get my head around why this Hymer was 52 grand as against the Benimar on the stand next door at 30 grand. Asking the salesman, he replied with an unjustified arrogance, well, it's quality, isn't it? Before turning away, still perplexed, I asked, like what? Looking at me with a slight sneer he found hard to disguise, he dismissively waved his arms at the sofas and said, "well, the coverings, for instance." Seeing my gormless expression, he followed up with, "these motorhomes have 40m insulation. You can go up into the arctic in one of these."

It was then I lost my temper; I ain't looking for a motorhome to travel up into the f***ing arctic, I thought before walking out. Completely lost, baffled, and mystified, we walked out and gave up. And these salesmen get paid a lot of money? We spent another year at least looking around. Slowly, inexorably, we found out what worked and what didn't. The Benimar was a new start-up Spanish company that, seeing the increasing demand, jumped on the bandwagon and built motorhomes. Where the Hymer salesman was right was in the fact that the Benimar was poorly put together. We later found many owners moaning about the poor quality and numerous faults. Clearly, we had had a lucky escape. It would have helped if the idiot Hymer salesman had been a bit more honest and less arrogant.

We found the Hymer hideous and very bland. We found this because of the German tendency for quality over looks; it seems all Germans insisted on a Mercedes engine. The motorhome business is a minefield. We were totally ignorant. First, there are so many manufacturers, then so many models, and within the models, so many layouts. Initially, like most people we later found, we were terrified; we were not talking a couple of grand here but 30—40 grand upwards, and it seemed no one was very helpful. One helpful nugget was the one salesman advising us to be very careful and recalling one customer who bought a layout with bunk beds that were totally unsuitable and cost him a right few quid to exchange. It was a salutary lesson that we took on board.

Slowly we narrowed it down to about three models and makes and one layout. Then to two models, the Auto trail Chieftain and the Auto trail Cheyenne. The Chieftain was beautiful. But it was about six feet longer than the Cheyenne and a good few grand dearer. We spent some time passing from one to the other before going for the Cheyenne; the chieftain was a six-wheel – more expense. Inside, it took us a bit to realise and justify the extra expense; we had chosen a design layout that we thought was ideal for us, trying to imagine every scenario. Coming off the beach, we chose two sofas, big enough to put our feet up and have a nap without having to get into bed, two feet shorter than the Chieftain. They were still five feet long, plenty long enough. Fixed bed to the back running side to side with a garage underneath that made another two-foot difference. The rest comprised the toilet and shower room, with an outside shower and BBQ point. We thought we had made the best and wisest choice; it was the SE model, so it came with a built-in rear camera, great, with a built-in television which was useless. A 7-inch television! Yet another bonus that I only appreciated much later was the fiat 2.8 turbo diesel engine.

Time proved we had made the right choice. The garage was a godsend, as was the fixed bed. Whilst travelling, Bet could get into bed and go to sleep on a long journey. Tired, we could pull in, settle in for the night, jump into bed and go straight to sleep. With a bit of practice, we were ready for our adventures.

THE FIRST FOOTSTEPS

Our plan from the outset was simple, to enjoy the summers in England, travelling to wherever took our fancy. Whilst we're not gipsies, we did like the idea of the freedom of the road. We were totally self-contained with a nice gas fire, a three-way fridge, gas, battery and 240v, and a good quality gas cooker with one electric hob if we were on a site. We were to find out about the sites, but being fully self-contained, our plan was to wild camp; we thought it would be simple,

We lived in Birmingham, well, the posh part really, Sutton Coldfield, so we were middle class. Well, pretend middle class because I actually grew up in Aston and Nechells, but I've learned to pronounce my words with the capital A as in 'bAth'. Anyway, enough about me. For all the people who run Birmingham down, I can tell you it's a friendly place to be. Brummies' are easy going and like to get on with their lives, but the big advantage is it's central to everywhere.

To many of us, Birmingham is the beating heart of the country. Well, until Hitler got to work on us. Our city fathers, in their wisdom, did the rest. They knocked down and destroyed many beautiful architectural buildings. Now it's a job to find any. The odd house or building around the city centre, the old bull ring knocked down (that wasn't destroyed by bombs). Now, unlike London and York, only a few buildings of character remain. The old crown in Digbeth has existed since circa 1366, keeping its old black and white

9

timber frame and has survived civil wars to become grade 11 listed. Originally a staging post for travellers, it was one of the first sights seen by farmers bringing their sheep, cattle and pigs down to the slaughterhouse. In the 1960s, the city fathers destroyed the city centre building a new gaudy monstrosity smack bang by Saint Martin's church comprising cheap plastic covers over the barrow boys selling their wares.

Many of the old inner city houses and so-called slums were destroyed in a mad post-war blitz, giving no thought to the loss of character and community, rebuilding monstrous ugly multi-story flats and modern houses that quickly became slums themselves.

Thankfully, they finally woke up and rebuilt the city centre in later years, bringing it into the twentieth century. The city centre throbbed with excitement when they rebuilt it in later years and brought it into the twentieth century. Certain areas or sections are set aside for the public to enter and fish from the pools.

In between Sutton park and Birmingham, in Aston Hall. A beautiful Jacobean mansion built by Sir Thomas Holt circa 1618-1635. Packed to the rafters with architectural gems and historical treasures, including the great oak staircase, which still shows battle scars of the English civil war, set in its own beautiful grounds. It is only spoilt by the slums around it and the ugly vista of Aston Villa Football Club. At one stage, it would have stood alone on a mound overlooking Birmingham's City Centre and the countryside. Of course, there are one or two other places of historic interest around Birmingham, but they are few and far between. At some cost, the council renovated a few mid-terrace Victorian houses on Hurst Street as museum pieces. For want of a bit of thought, they could have retained entire communities in blocks of mid-terrace and back-to-backs that many people would have been proud to

still live in. Instead, they demolished them and replaced them with bigger slums. Mind, I don't think it helped by bringing in millions of diverse ethnic peoples from different parts of the world, unsettling and altering the very social fabric of our society that has been adjusting and growing over two thousand years. And before you start, there is nothing racist in that comment.

Now, a way of life enjoyed by millions can only be enjoyed by visiting the black country living museum in Dudley, a fantastic award-winning living museum set on some 26 landscaped acres. If you want to see Victorian Birmingham, go there. These were communities where families were born, lived and died, and then their children continued the tradition, all growing up and knowing each other. That has all been ripped up and taken away from us, but the true Brummie friendliness still survives – barely.

It's 120 miles to London, full of cockneys (some say gobby cockneys, but not me) and posers. It's 90 miles to Manchester, full of football players who are always moaning about the rain. We are 90 miles to the nearest coast, some say shorter, Weston-super-Mare being a mere 110 miles or so. Barmouth about equal distance and full of the welsh moaning about the many English who live there. London is nearer to Kent and the south coast, but you have to live in London to want to travel there, say no more.

At any rate, you get my drift; we live in a very convenient position to get anywhere. Even the ferries in Portsmouth are only 160 miles, a three-hour steady drive.

For our first drive out, we headed for Weston-Super-Mare and a campsite. Eventually, we obviously wanted to wild camp but felt it best to test the waters slowly and gently. Weston is a pleasant town, always popular with Brummies' because of its accessibility. A quick hour on the motorway by car or coach and you're on the beach, even sooner if you go to Brean. It's also a pleasant town to explore. The beach road runs right through from the golf club to Kewstoke, some two or three miles of flat walking. Opposite the seafront are the various hotels, guest houses and the town centre, a very attractive shopping centre worth a visit in its own right with a nice easy, relaxed atmosphere.

Finding somewhere to park in our motorhome was a mission in itself. Great during the day. For five quid, we could park on the sandy beach where we could put out our table and chairs, but no overnight parking. They have it sussed those Weston councillors. Even the disabled badge holders were limited to two hours. Plenty enough time to spend your money, then bugger off somewhere else or pay extra. Coming off the beach, we passed another motorhome, and when I enquired about parking overnight, he cheerfully shouted, "I don't go on sites. I'd rather spend my money touring and sightseeing." Seemed quite sensible to me, but where to park?

Along the seafront, to Kewstoke, I noticed a little forest or a clump of trees to the right. Seeing a space, I did a quick about-turn, pulled in and put the kettle on. Getting the wine out, I thought, right, let's have a little snort. Before my second slurp, I was interrupted by a guy in a landrover. "You can't park here."

Puzzled, I asked, "why not?"

"It's just not allowed. If you're still here in one hour, we will have to inform the police." Well, we can't argue with that. Without further ado and with the time marching on, we found the nearest campsite at the far end of the beach road towards the golf club right on the seafront. A little gem and well worth the few pounds it cost for the night. We had a few nights. What a lovely place. A pleasant walk to the town centre and amenities. The price was reasonable as well, but the first of my little niggles started to eat into my little brainbox. I was happy enough to pay a reasonable price for a pitch with a first-class position adjoining the beach, but these types of campsites were few and far between. Besides, we were self-sufficient.

For the odd one or two nights, fine, but what about the longer term? All we were really paying for was the privilege of being on a site. Yes, there were facilities, but we had those facilities on board. Buying a caravan is one thing. You can't just park up anywhere in a caravan, but in a motorhome, you can lock your doors and put your head down. This is a phenomenon that various councils were taking a long time to wake up to.

It was and still continues to be a big learning curve. We joined the caravan and camping club only to find they were, in many cases, more expensive than many private campsites, and these are supposed to be charity-run. How do they get around this? Where does all the money go? In eye-watering salaries to those few at the top, that's where. Charities are the new go-to for guaranteed top money. Get a job in charity or set your own up, and you're made for life.

The camping and caravan club have a nice little offshoot in the form of the CLs. These are little sites around the country offering basic facilities for only five vans under the umbrella of the club itself. That means they can't operate alone. Cheap, they ain't always cheerful. Many campers join them just for the CLs. We booked into one in Kewstoke just the far side of Weston-super-Mare, just a few hundred yards to the beach. It was owned by an ex-army major or captain, and the site was in his orchard, overgrown and amongst apple trees. It was pleasant if you liked that kind of thing. Adequate for a couple of nights, maybe longer in the season. Cheap as it was, the major/captain valued his little income, panicking when a sixth caravanner turned up to claim his spot.

We were turned out unceremoniously, spots like these were great if you wanted peace and solitude for a cheap price, but we found after trying various places for a year it wasn't for us. Some of the best places to pitch up were in the country, and we discovered we could park up for very little or free, anyway.

Another minor disappointment we found, and at first, I thought it was me, was that caravan owners didn't put themselves out or be friendly to motorhome owners. Many motorhome owners, usually couples, preferred to keep themselves to themselves. That's why they bought the motorhome or even caravan. If they wanted to be friendly, they would go to a hotel. Silly Billy, it would have been nice just to say hello or good afternoon. No, if they wanted company, they preferred to come away in groups of two or more or meet up on-site.

We found that owning a motorhome and finding what suited us was almost as bad as fighting your way through a relationship. You think you've found a suitable partner, but it's sometimes mind-sapping, enervating, and frustrating. We were thirty miles from Stourport. To us Brummies, it was known as Stourport on Sea because it was our nearest resort for a day out. Any bank holiday, and we would get the Midland red bus for a great day out in the town. Set on the banks of the river Severn and downstream from Bewdley and Holt Fleet, the town was the go-to place for all Brummies and black country people intent on having a cheap and enjoyable time on the one side of the road that ran through the town and sitting alongside the river, was the fair that sat permanently open. On the other side of the fair, the Basin and berths for boats and barges.

Some of the older properties here, like the grain store overlooking the river, had been converted into luxury apartments, along with other properties that were built or converted. Together with the live aboard, barges and canal boats started to transform and have a beneficial impact on the town.

On the opposite side of the river were the campsites full mainly of cheap and cheerful caravans brought on-site by people from Birmingham and the black country for a weekend or longer break and a good pee up and game of bingo in the clubhouse. Here you could get a pitch for the night for a few quid.

Heading up the river and under the main road bridge lay fields and spaces for games, football concerts and other forms of entertainment, plenty enough to entertain anyone coming into the town for a day out. Further, along with less than a mile of nice steady walking along the river bank, you came to the Lickhill caravan site. For some reason, they boasted this as a David Bellamy award-winning site and thus justifying an increase in nightly camping fees. Having spent a couple of nights there, we just couldn't see the justification in price. It was just a field. The top half is for caravans and motorhomes, the bottom half for tents, tidy but still a mowed field.

Up river from Stourport sat Bewdley three miles further on. A town established in the 14th century. A destination point for all boats and barges bringing goods up one of the busiest rivers in Europe. Here they were offloaded and delivered by packhorse to Wales and the black country. In its early days, Bewdley was a thriving town, but slowly the wealth deteriorated over the years. Still, a lovely place to visit for a day or two. It was full of historic and medieval houses, shops and buildings. On the opposite side of the river lay a small untidy field owned and let out to campers who came away for a few hours fishing along the banks of the river. I had the impression that the owner had maybe given up on the field due to a lack of business or maybe an unwillingness by some campers to pay the fees. It was for that reason we started using the car park adjoining the river, which we found ideal as it was just a few minutes' walk along the river bank. For a small fee, we could park up overnight and enjoy a night in the town in one of its lovely pubs accompanied by a portion of fish-n-chips from its excellent award-winning chippy, eaten at one of the tables adjoining the river.

Bewdley became a regular venue until one time, we turned up only to find they had put height barriers across the entrance. With nowhere else to pitch up in such proximity to the town, we felt stymied. Seeing the traffic warden, I asked him why the barriers had been put up. After some consideration, he slowly told us it was because of the gipsies. Apparently, a group of them had turned up, as they do, and made the car park their home. It cost the small town of Bewdley a great deal of money to get them evicted, then a further £2,000 to clean up the rubbish and excrement they had left.

The warden was obviously a tad angry about the whole thing and informed me that the council were working with other councils and the government to find a way to put a stop to it. The problem is still that the gipsies are now a protected race. God knows how this came about, but it seems yet another example of how free speech and democracy are being high-jacked in this country.

Why France doesn't seem to have this problem with its Aires, I don't know, but it was, we found, a continuing problem. Further up the river lay Holt Fleet, another pleasant little place to spend a few hours or a day. One day we called into the pub across the bridge and adjoining the river. Parking up, I called into the pub and spoke to a member of staff asking if we could spend the night on the far side of the car park, our intention being to have a meal and a few drinks. Heading off behind the bar, she came back a few seconds later, telling us with a smile that the manager had agreed that we could stop the night.

Getting into bed for a quick nap, we were disturbed just a few minutes later by frantic banging on the cab door. The same woman staff member was panic stricken. "I'm so sorry," she stuttered, "but the boss said you can't stop here. You must go." We could see from her attitude that it was no good pleading or arguing with her. We were out on our ear. Obviously, it was because of the gipsy problem; I surmised. From their viewpoint, we could have been gipsies or just as bad a magnet for other gipsies seeing us on site. It was getting beyond a joke.

We initially intended to alternate between local venues interspersed with more distant places to visit, learning as we went along what to take with us, what was/is essential, and what was only useful occasionally. Our bathroom cupboard was stacked with every toiletry that we kept in our house. We just replicated and added extras, toothbrushes, soap shampoos etc. and, of course, not forgetting toilet paper. A container of medicines, bandages, aspirin, paracetamol, creams etc., plus many other things that may be useful.

Our wardrobe was kitted out with every item of clothing that we anticipated using; short-sleeved shirts, slacks, shorts, and swimming trunks. Our cupboards, and we had plenty besides the garage and under-bed storage, were filled with all manner of things that we could think of, from a toolkit to superglue. Our food cupboards were equally so, with long-life tins of hams, pork luncheon meats, to tinned pies that made a meal after twenty minutes in the oven. We quickly decided that we didn't want to use our cold water tanks for drinking water. Many people did and saw no harm in it, though. Containing 80 litres, we preferred to use the water for showering and washing, carrying a four-gallon container for fresh drinking water. Fussy, we were not, but we both like to see where our fresh water is coming from. We quickly found out that whilst it seemed to take ages to fill the tank, it emptied in double quick time.

A motorhome is a bit of a personal thing. You buy what suits you and hope you have made the right purchase; we felt after a great deal of thought and consideration, we had made the right choice. At circa 22ft, our Cheyenne was plenty big enough for us to relax and spread out on the sofas. It was also ideal for those times when the kids and grandchildren spent some time with us.

The very thought of buying one of the smaller VW-type pop-ups was a no-go before the start. Yet some purpose-built were even more expensive than our Cheyenne. Why would you want to buy something so small? On one campsite outside Oxford, we couldn't help but observe a couple on a nearby pitch. While it was raining, we could see them huddled up over the table, passing the time by playing cards before having to make the bed up and get into it.

The next morning, the rain had stopped, and they sat outside huddled up in heavy coats drinking from a cup. No, no, no, not for us, I'm afraid. At 18—20 with your girlfriend, up close and comfortable, great. At fifty-plus, no. We felt the move not to go bigger was the right one. We met one couple with a beauty; it was at least 30 ft long with slide-out sides and a levelling ramp underneath.

Approaching it whilst admiring it, the guy admitted he wished he had brought smaller. We were in a car park by choice. Not being able to find a campsite to take him, he had to resort to ringing the local council, who advised him to stop in the car park. These big ones were great for the American and Australian roads, but our little island was not so much. The idea of touring those narrow lanes around Cornwall would give us nightmares.

There was nothing clever about our choice. As time went along, I just felt we were lucky in the choice we had made. It wasn't great on diesel. With a two-point eight turbo diesel, it only managed 20mpg, but that was offset by other benefits. Besides, you don't treat a motorhome like a car.

SPREADING OUR WINGS

Our initial plans were straightforward, first to enjoy the summers meandering around England, Wales and Scotland. A short two or three days around England and Wales, with a much longer period, allowed for Scotland and the scenic north coast NC500, covering some 500 miles. But, as they say, the best-laid plans etc., and we were finding wild camping a big learning curve.

For those just wishing to spend their holiday breaks on campsites, it was and is quite straightforward. As well as the recognised camp sites like the caravan and camping club, there are many private camp sites dotted around the country, prices dictated by position and demand. It is simply a matter of where you want to go, Barmouth, Torquay, or Weston-Super-Mare.

Many motorhome owners simply use their campers for a weekend, annual or fortnightly break. If you've got three or four kids, a campsite with all facilities can work out relatively cheap, well cheaper than a five-star hotel, I suppose, but then you have to consider the initial cost of the motorhome, many of which can cost as much as a house or more. To spend fifty grand or more on a motorhome works out at five grand a year, plus the cost of the holiday itself over ten years.

Families understandably use the campsites for the facilities. If our grandchildren or children joined us, we would book into a campsite. Elderly people choose campsites for security, which is understandable, especially if you're only popping out for the odd weekend or weeks' break. Drive around many motorhome owners' houses throughout the year, and you will see motorhomes parked up, week in week out. To my mind, if I was going to do that, I'd buy a caravan. To pay such a lot of money for a motorhome only to have it sitting on your drive for much of the year just didn't make sense.

Our plan was to spend much of the year touring and visiting places of interest, both here and abroad. With some prices at £250 per week plus, that knocks a hole in it. Some £6,000 over six months, all that to just sit in a field. For any pensioner or family, that is a lot of money. In many cases equal to the average pension for a couple.

Many of us set out the same way, in total ignorance of where to go, how to camp, where to camp, and where to tip our waste water or cassette. We were no different. Looking at the map, we would pick somewhere with a pin and say, 'let's go there'. Brixham seemed a cheerful place to visit, with a beautiful harbour and town. The only problem was there was nowhere to park a motorhome in or by Brixham. We could get in the small car park for a few hours, but not overnight. This was another recent phenomenon we were to get used to, in big letters accompanied by a picture of the camper van, just in case you're a bit thick and can't read, 'No overnight camping'. It was becoming quite clear. Come in a car, stop in a hotel, spend your money, then go home. Some camper and motorhome sites are great for advice, overnight parking, pub stop overs, etc. Some really seem to scrape the barrel. Great overnight stay near such-and-such a town, two miles out of a layby off the 33, fairly quiet and not too noisy at night. Christ, we're not gipsies.

Keen to explore Brixham, we drove around to find somewhere to spend the night. After a tiring day, we came across a very quiet, out of the way, industrial site.

Perfect. Pulling in, we settled down for the night, only to be mortified when we were woken by a lot of noise. The quiet place that we had chosen was now bustling with life, vehicles coming in and out, and people milling around. We couldn't get out of there quick enough. We put Brixham in the rear-view mirror and headed off to Torquay, 8 miles along the road.

Between Brixham and Torquay was Paignton; the three collectively known as the English Riviera. Just outside Paignton was the vast leisure centre and car park. Down in the bottom corner were a couple of motorhomes, one a Cheyenne like ours. Speaking to the two families ensconced there, they told us that there was no problem spending the night as long as we purchased a ticket. It was clear even the fairground owners stored their equipment there. It was quite easy to travel or even get the bus into Paignton for a pleasant day on the beach or mooching around the town.

From Paignton, we could drive into Torquay or Brixham with ease, returning at night for a relaxing night in a secure position. A place to put into our little book for future use. Slowly but surely, we could build up some nice free or fairly cheap places to park.

Just a short drive from Paignton, we came into Teignmouth, a great place for a family holiday and many family-friendly activities and things to do. After making some enquiries, we were told it would be fine to park up overnight on the main seafront car park as the attendant only attended in the week. As it was the weekend, we tried it for two nights.

Teignmouth has everything for the family, a long expanse of nice sandy beach, a lido, pier and play park, plus arcades for you to spend even more money. A delightful town with its own British charm, its name coming from the river Teign. Candy-coloured beach huts lined the beach along with blue and white striped deck chairs on the town, enjoyed as much by the locals as by the tourist visitors. Boats line the harbour with plenty of restaurants serving fresh seafood, pasties and fish-n-chips. Views from the Teign estuary are a fantastic way to see the sunset and sunrise. Or along the Victorian pier where you can spend your money in the slot machines. To stroll along the seafront with an ice cream bought from one of its iconic upturned cornets was a delight or a sausage sandwich from the east cliff café. If you manage to get bored with all that, you can catch a train which stops off at a number of great places east or west.

The beach is great for swimming being calm, except by the river mouth opening, or you can catch the passenger ferry and spend a few hours visiting Shaldon and its pubs and cafes. For a longer walk, you can head out along the headland, past Smugglers' Lane, to neighbouring Dawlish. With its main shopping streets and back allies, there are plenty of shops and galleries, including the local artist Laura Wall who specialises in Teignmouth and local places.

Another delightful visitor attraction is Clun, a small, beautiful village in the Shropshire hills. When you visit Clun, you are stepping back in time to one of the most tranquil and peaceful villages in the country. Within the village and nearby the brook running through the town is Clun Castle, a medieval ruined castle built and established in the 11th century by the Norman Lord, Robert de Say, after the Norman invasion of England. It became an important marcher lord castle with an extensive and imposing castle guard system.

Clun Castle itself stands above the town and can be accessed by a wooden footbridge that crosses the river. Further along and leading into the small picturesque market square sits the 15th-century stone bridge crossing river Clun. Alongside the river lies a free car park with well-maintained toilets at one end near the wooden footbridge. Parked up in a discreet corner of the car park, listening to the rush of the river was a delight. In the summer, we could see children playing in the water. Above and behind the town was yet another free car park giving immediate access to the town, Spar store and a delightful couple of pubs serving good food. Apart from the castle, river, and town, there were many hiking trails and bike treks. A truly lovely place to visit for a short one or two maximum overnight stays.

Just a short drive from Clun stood Wroxeter, or Viriconium, to give it its Roman name. Wroxeter is a 2000-year-old Roman city, once the fourth largest in Roman Britain. Run by English heritage, it comprises the bathhouse and a reconstructed town house rebuilt following methods used over 2000 years ago. Once almost as large as Pompeii, it gives an insight into Roman living with an audio tour of the city.

Arriving late afternoon, we spent the night in the large open car park adjoining the museum before paying a small entrance fee and touring it the next day. It was quite amazing to stand there amongst the grounds and ruins, trying to envisage a life as it was 2000 years ago, as a bustling city full of people. Steam baths and theatres and, more interestingly, Roman toilets running in a line. It wasn't too difficult to imagine those Romans sitting there doing their business, having a chat, putting the world to rights and using a shared sponge to wipe themselves after they had finished. After dipping in a handy tub of water, of course. Yikes. The question that came to my mind was, 'where did the Roman ladies do their business?' Did they sit and squat next to the men, or did they have their own separate rows of toilets? The mind boggles. A great and interesting day out.

As well as being a nice place to live, Birmingham is a great hub with spokes leading out to all parts of the country. Within a short distance of 40 or 50 miles, we could be in a pleasant area to spend a few days or longer.

Cannock Chase was one such delightful place to stay, just twenty miles from our home in Sutton Coldfield. Formally a royal forest, it has been designated as an area of outstanding natural beauty run by the forestry commission. It is also one of the biggest natural forests in England. The chase has something for everyone, from hiking and walking to cycling trails. It also has three campsites, one run by the camping and caravan club in an idyllic location, set behind a very nice café with outdoor seating. Another, privately owned and run by a farm, basically just sitting within a not-very-attractive field. The only benefit is electricity.

The best, by far, is Takaroo, a natural campsite set within the forest and run by the Forestry Commission, the cheapest of all three sites. The site is at its most basic, with tipping facilities for waste dotted about a communal rubbish disposal point and water taps. Why it isn't far more popular is beyond me, not that I'm complaining. Sitting outside our camper, it was almost like being in a different world. The sound of traffic was unnoticeable. At night, with everyone settled down and with little movement, wild deer and boar would walk freely around the forest and in front of you. Coming from the city, it was a sight and experience to behold. The only problem I found was that the forestry commission seemed to open and close at will. It is wise to check with them online before turning up.

Being impulsive, I would often forget. One such time in the low season and feeling like a break, I turned up and typically found it closed. At a loss what the actual law is on wild camping on the Chase, I found somewhere suitable to settle in for the night. There are literally dozens of car parks on Cannock Chase, some visible on the main roads running through and others on the beaten track. One was a car park running off and beyond another car park set off on one of the side roads. Turning in and nestling into the corner discreetly out of sight, I settled down with a cup of coffee. Door open. Apart from the odd straggler bringing their dog in for a walk, the place was desolate, ideal. My plan was to enjoy some walks across the forest whilst at night watching a bit of telly, reading or doing a bit of writing — bliss.

The only problem was it seemed to get busier at night. From eight o'clock onwards, more and more people kept turning up. Obviously walking their dogs. Only stepping out, I couldn't see any dogs. Come one o'clock in the morning, people were still pulling into the clearing and parking up. I couldn't figure it out. It was only on the second night when a car pulled in beside me, a little close, perhaps, considering it was such a decent-sized car park. Getting out with my binoculars, I said 'hello' to the guy in the car, and after a little chat, he pointed out that I was in a favourite dogging site. A dogging site!! Of course, it didn't help that I'd got my binoculars out did it. Apparently, I was on one of the less busy sites. The most popular one being further along and opposite the café. I was mortified. He then pointed out that it was a wonder that no couples had approached me (maybe wishing to share my van). Course, I never stopped to consider what he was doing on the site, and so close to me.

After considering my options, I realised that with doggers pulling in all night long and dog owners all day, I wouldn't be likely to be hassled or robbed and decided to stay put. With that in mind, I stopped and had another pleasant two nights. Whether I go back again is another matter.

WALES AND THE BORDERS

Shrewsbury and the welsh borders are less than fifty miles away and the gateway to Wales itself. Wales, the hills and mountains have always appealed to me, the natural ruggedness and beauty a joy to explore. The problem with Wales is the roads.

From Sutton, it's just a quick run onto the M6, and then it's a convenient motorway all the way to the M54. From Shrewsbury, it's B roads onwards. I have long suspected that the Welsh have deliberately not improved the road network to make it difficult for us English to get anywhere. From Sutton to Shrewsbury, it's a pleasant hours' drive. From Shrewsbury to Welshpool, a mere 19 miles, it's another hour's drive, and from Welshpool to Barmouth and the coast, another two hours' drive, and that's with no traffic hold-ups. So a drive to Barmouth from Sutton, some 119 miles, takes almost four hours.

Shrewsbury, the county town of Shropshire, is a place of beauty and interest, sitting inside a loop of the River Severn, its Tudor centre lined with half-timbered houses, the medieval red brick Shrewsbury castle houses, and the Shropshire regimental museum, full of military artefacts, uniforms and weaponry. There are many places of interest to visit, including St Chad's church with its circular nave and St Mary's church with its beautiful and elaborate stained glass windows. Unspoilt, the town centre still keeps its medieval street plan with some 600 plus listed buildings and many examples of timber buildings. Shrewsbury Abbey was founded in 1074 by the Norman Earl of Shrewsbury, Roger De Montgomery, for its Benedictine monks. It's also known as the birthplace of Charles Darwin.

The town was the early capital of the kingdom of Powys, known to early Britain as Schrosberie, which eventually became Shrewsbury. Originally the site of many conflicts between the English and the Welsh King Offa, it is only a few miles from Wroxeter and the fourth largest Roman city. Gifted to Roger De Montgomery by William, it was he who built the castle and fortified the town. Also famous for its wool production during the middle ages trading with the rest of Europe through its access from the River Severn and Watling Street.

The black death devastated the town in the mid-1300s, and in the early 1400s fought a losing battle with King Henry IV. Later Henry VIII intended to make Shrewsbury a cathedral city, but the inhabitants refused the offer. The town is also famous for its Ditherington Flax Mill, completed in 1797, the world's first iron-framed building commonly regarded as the grandfather of the modern skyscraper, eventually becoming a grade I listed building.

The new ring road saved some of the historic houses from demolition in the early 1960s. Attacked by the IRA in 1992, they detonated a bomb within Shrewsbury castle, causing significant damage to its museum. From the late 1990s, large swathes of the town were flooded, leaving much of the town underwater. Since then, the flooding has been less severe but still leaves the town car parks under water, preventing shoppers from getting into town. Shrewsbury is well worth visiting and makes a lovely and interesting day or two out. I found it quite easy to park near the centre of the town in my motorhome. Certainly, it's a place I would visit again. Well, come to think of it, most of the places I visited I would visit again.

19 miles further west, we arrived in Welshpool, famous for its cattle market and four miles in from the Welsh border and low-lying on the River Severn. Its Welsh name – Y TRALLWNG, means marshy or sinking land. Welshpool is a great place to explore Wales. Lined with fine Georgian buildings, many built of brick, brought in by the Montgomery Canal or the River Severn. The hexagonal building tucked away behind Broad street is a very rare cockfighting ring.

To the edge of Welshpool lies the Welshpool and Llanfair light railway. You can ride this narrow-gauge railway from Raven Square to Llanfair Caereinion, a 16-mile round trip taking about 45 minutes each way. A trip not to be missed. I have a soft spot for this part of Wales as I worked on a mixed agricultural farm in nearby Llanymynech, some 6 miles away. Wales, I loved. Working six days a week, sometimes seven, for three quid a week, I did not. Running into the centre of Welshpool is the Montgomery Canal, bringing wildlife and aquatic plants, otters and water voles. Kingfishers can also be seen. From here and along the towpath, you can take a leisurely stroll to Newtown, just nine miles away, yet another interesting town. Welshpool is also in the top ten per cent of places to live, according to Royal Mail. If you walk around it, you can see why with its delightful tea rooms and cafes.

The cattle market is a must if you can find time to visit. Drawing farmers from all around the area, bringing in cattle and sheep and wildfowl to buy and sell. One of my delights used to be travelling on the back of a tractor into town to witness the auctioneers doing their selling. Oswestry, another market and railway town with the Montgomery Canal running through, is some 15 miles away, with Llanymynech in between. Established some 3000 years ago in Shropshire, England, at the junction of the A5. I used to alternate my days off between the two, Welshpool being my favourite. Both towns have plenty to see and do, with historic castles and museums and houses nearby. Just a

short twenty-five miles north of Welshpool lies the pretty village
of Llangollen and the Pontcysyllte Aqueduct, both well worth a
visit. I always consider Welshpool the gateway to west, south,
and even north Wales, though in truth, to reach Rhyl and
Llandudno, I usually whizz up the M6 and do a left at Broughton.

Heading out of Welshpool, it is a matter of choice whether
to carry on west to Barmouth and the seaside or south down
to Pembroke. Each has its own beauty. Pembroke is yet
another pretty town with its imposing castle, the birthplace of
Henry VII. Strictly speaking, you cannot wild camp overnight
in the car park by the castle, but telling the landlady of the
nearby corner pub I wanted a drink, she informed me that no
one came round after six pm, so I would be perfectly safe to
have a drink and stop overnight. She was right, and I did,
shhhhh. Thankfully, I find Wales quite accommodating
towards the camper. Most of the time. Though obviously, it's a
matter of being respectful at all times. That means parking
carefully and with consideration, not being a complete idiot
and leaving rubbish around or worse, and I have heard the
odd story. Yes, disgraceful as it is, it has and happens. Usually,
I suspect by people who don't have onboard facilities. At all
times, it's don't overstay and only leave footprints.

Thirty-five miles further west, which seems like triple that
along those B roads, lies the lovely little town of Dolgellau.
Known for its annual July music festival, Dolgellau is a hidden
gem with over 230 stone houses on urban conservation lists.
With its narrow streets and quaint shops, once known for its
textile industry signs, it remains with its high-up doors and
pulley systems. Small round windows at the top of buildings
denote the hidden meeting houses of the Quakers. Where to
park? Well, just a few yards outside the town is the main car
park, where I have been given permission to park in low
season as long as you buy a ticket. Another welcoming place
is the rugby club car park further back. From there, a very

pleasant little café selling ice creams is ideal for freshening up with a coffee before heading into town for a little mooch.

With a couple of friendly pubs and cafes, there are plenty of places to sit and people-watch. One time, going for the Welsh breakfast, I was a bit stymied about what the difference was between the Welsh breakfast to the English. A short distance from Dolgellau lies the River Mawddach and Cader Idris, where many people come to climb along its three main paths. If you don't fancy climbing that there are dozens of less challenging mountain trails offering different views of the area. I usually give Cader a miss, I'm afraid.

A few miles from Dolgellau lies Machynlleth, yet another pretty town, just up in the mountains between Machynlleth and Llanidloes and just above the reservoir at Dylife lies the Star Pub. Anywhere around, there is a great place to spend a peaceful few nights with the odd drink in the pub. Totally isolated, it makes for a great place to chill. Or visit some of the local towns or villages like Tywyn or Fairbourne, small seaside resorts along the coast. Together with many of the places inland, there are places where it's quite acceptable to park up or at least tolerated.

At Fairbourne itself, there are a few places to camp up overnight, but for anyone of a timid nature or perhaps feeling the need for more security, the local golf club allows you to park within its grounds for a small fee. From here, you can get the model railway along the beach road over the estuary and into Barmouth for a small fee. The ride was a delight, with amazing views. It is a simple choice between stopping in Fairbourne and getting the return train to Barmouth or vice versa. Personally, if I go to Barmouth, I prefer to stay at least two or three days with a half-day visit to Fairbourne.

Many pubs around England and Wales, especially with good-sized car parks, will allow you to stay overnight if you spend a few quid in the pub. The only problem with this is the lines between spending become a bit blurred between you and the publican. If you just go in and buy a pint, then retire to your camper, they might think you're taking the Michael. If there are two of you or even a family of four, and you feel obliged to buy a meal, it can be a very expensive overnight stay. I tend not to ask or stop. If I eat out, I like the idea of free choice. Barmouth itself has been a favourite place to visit for years, from past times in a leaky tent to a caravan on the beachfront. Now I find it's a great place to spend two or three days with the grandkids. Once, we tried Rhyl, where I had found a nice place to park right on the seafront behind a pub and next to the Holiday Inn, free, of course. Unfortunately, Rhyl is not the most salubrious of places to visit or stay. The hotels are run down and unappealing; you have the impression that most of the town is unemployed and on the dole. Sadly, having been in the hotel business ourselves, we found the British seaside resorts were just not catching up with the times. Who is going to spend a great deal of money when, in many cases, they can get a package deal to Spain for a fortnight with the guaranteed sun for the price of a week in England?

Now, many hotels and holiday flats have found it more lucrative to let rooms to the unemployed, the rent guaranteed and regular. The only problem is it brings in all the undesirables from all over the country who don't want to work. I know because I was guilty of it myself getting into the rental business.

Contrast Rhyl with Llandudno, just a few miles further along, clean, welcoming with grand hotels kept in excellent condition. Talking to the locals, they also make it very clear how aware they are, only in the main employing from the local labour pool. Blackpool is an even worse example. The glory days of Blackpool have long gone, with far too many hotels, guest houses and letting flats turned over to the DHSS. What staggered me even more, was the number of drunks and drug addicts there were in the town. The first time we ever visited was for my wife's birthday, never having been to Blackpool before. It was an eye-opener.

Drunks just wondered the streets. Drug addicts hung around, and the street vendors were visibly sharp and watchful. I couldn't get my head around it until I discovered that drug addicts and alcoholics are now treated as sick or disabled. This is great intelligence of the government, you have to admit. So you drink, you become an alcoholic; you take drugs; you become a drug addict. Being sick and disabled, you are entitled to more benefits, of course, and with more benefits, you can therefore buy more booze and drugs, ha-ha, great, *ay*? These are government officials running our country.

With a funfair in Rhyl, I thought my kids would like it. A nice long beach, plenty of shops. But no, they took one look around and decided they wanted out. After just a few hours, we got back into the motorhome and set off quick sharpish to Barmouth. My grandkids were sharper than me.

Barmouth was a big contrast, again a nice beach, a pleasant town to walk around and a nice small fair. A good quality fish-n-chip shop to boot. Barmouth had gone through a bad patch many years earlier with run-down hotels, cafes and shops, but its saving grace possibly was its limited supply of hotels and guest houses. I suspect the Barmouth Council woke up to the potential problems and started turfing them out. The only problem I found with Barmouth was their unpredictability to the motorhome owner. Upon first visiting Barmouth, we would drive to the very far end of the beachfront road out of town. This road runs a very good distance, perhaps close to a mile, with car parks virtually all the way along. For most of the year, mostly empty. During our first year in the motorhome, we got chatting with the local traffic warden, who informed us that as long as we bought a ticket, a blind eye was turned to us spending overnight. At the cost of some 6 pounds, I thought the council were getting the better of the deal. With no facilities except the distant toilets, who else was parking there?

The local kiosk owner would serve us a cup of tea, coffee or ice cream for a small charge whilst proudly telling us how he had brought the kiosk, improved it and built the business up. Over the years, we would always pop in and say hello. How he survived, god knows. Initially, the far car park always had a few motorhomes parked up, but eventually, they fizzled out. The council put height restrictions in the second enormous car park. Was this a deliberate action? It seemed like it. We also heard one or two rumours that young locals had thrown paint or stones at the motorhomes. At any rate, I decided more and more to spend time in the large car park next to the lifeboat rescue centre. This was central to the town and its amenities. At the opposite end of the lifeboat station stood the town gaol, now disused. A stone-built circular building. It wasn't a pretty sight at all. Kept busy, mainly by the drunken sailors that came into the port and were thrown in for the night to sober up.

I wasn't alone. Quite a few other motorhome owners also spent a night or two spread around the car park. Having spent a couple of nights the previous week with no hassle, I was disappointed to wake up with the kids telling me I had got a ticket. Worse, a guy parked near the front had got a ticket as well, having asked me if it was safe to park there. I'd told him yes. Unfortunately, it was a bank holiday. Whilst the council or warden had turned a blind eye the previous night, we were now taking up a car parking space for day visitors. I was not a happy bunny at all, and without letting it spoil our break, I wrote a very strong letter to Gwynedd Council that ran the Barmouth Council. Some say that because Barmouth is known as little Birmingham because of the Brummy population that owned businesses there and Gwynedd is mostly Welsh, there is a bit of rivalry.

At any rate, in writing the letter, I made it very clear I wasn't going to pay any fine. Further, I pointed out that except for bank holidays, virtually all the car parks were permanently empty. The odd driver goes to the far end to do a bit of fishing. The near end is mainly used by locals. Large open spaces are left empty for months at a time. As a builder, I also made the point that for just a few hundred pounds, they could install a tap and waste tipping point. For that facility, they could charge a nominal ten pounds a night, which I am sure most motorhome owners would be happy to pay. Imagine the number of motorhome owners who would use the places once that was known.

It wouldn't impact the only campsite as they served mainly tents and caravans. Over three nights, I spent over three hundred pounds in the town on food and the funfair. At the very least, I would have thought most would spend a bit on food from the supermarket or having a drink in the local pubs. It doesn't take a lot of brains, does it? At any rate, I heard no further, so maybe the council, along with many other councils around the country, might shake up a bit.

The experience has put a little of a dampener on my once enjoyable visits to Barmouth. I don't think I'm the only camper van, or motorhome owner, to feel the same. I can drive into any resort in a car or estate car and spend many nights with no problem at all. Pull in with a camper, and the alarm bells go off.

Is it because a small minority dump rubbish or worse? Or is it because of the gipsy problem? They are terrified, like Bewdley, of letting one camper in for fear of another ten or twenty motorhomes sneaking in and setting up camp. The simple solution, ban the lot. How disgraceful, how discriminatory. How wrong. We have gone that far overboard; we are becoming more and more fearful of speaking our minds, upsetting a small minority in all walks of life, blacks, mixed race, gays, and lesbians. You name it, there is a discrimination ban. But what about us campers, us motor homers? How come Europe or France doesn't have this problem?

What tickles my funny bone is I don't think most of these gipsies, or itinerants, are real gipsy. They are tinkers, chancers, and Irish travellers looking to make money whilst living free wherever they can park up whilst touting for work cutting trees, tarmacking or garden work, all tax-free. Quite a few of them have homes, council homes back in Ireland, even here in England. Whilst the average guy goes out to work and earns £400 a week, he pays £100 in tax and insurance, £200 in rent and heating. He's left with £100 to buy his food. The traveller pays nothing or very little. They eat simply and cheaply. Pay nothing in rent and only have to worry about heating their caravan. If they charge £300 for a job, the almost full £300 pounds goes into his pocket.

They teach their kids the same way of life, giving them little education and aiming to let them leave school at the early age of 14. They have an inbuilt disrespect for us, who they call Gorgers. Whilst they call themselves Romany's. I have dealt with Romany's on a business basis, and I have seen them in a private capacity. Most people do not see that. When it comes to weddings or Christmas get-togethers, they have to find an alternative. After all, they can't hold a Christmas party in the caravan, can they, no matter how big?

For Christmas, they might book into holiday campsites or large hotels in small groups of three or four from different addresses. Once in, they will slowly integrate, and it is too late for the hosts to do anything about it. We had the misfortune to book into a holiday camp in Brean one Christmas and saw first-hand how they operate, much to the exasperation of the management and security. Fighting almost every night, admittedly amongst themselves. Deciding to hold a few weddings, six, I think, and probably running up against a brick wall. For venues, they chose Benidorm. Spreading out and around town, they booked into large hotels in small numbers, taking the hoteliers completely unawares. This might not be a problem, you might think, until they get their feet under the table. Slowly and gaining confidence, they spread out and relax. In doing so, they show their true selves. Gathered into large groups, fighting amongst themselves and just dropping food and litter around the restaurant and floors and around the swimming pool, the staff at their wits' end trying to keep them in check and tidy up after them. One or two hotels banned them from the hotel altogether. The corner bar in Benidorm tried all ways to accommodate them before giving up altogether and closing the place down. They were taking drugs and fighting regularly. Protected species, don't make me laugh.

Going through the town of Barmouth and along the back roads for eleven miles brings you to the small town of Harlech and Harlech Castle. Harlech is a seaside resort lying on Tremadog bay in the Snowdonia National Park. Harlech sits on a rocky crag overlooking the dunes and sea below, probably having one of the most spectacular settings for a castle built for and by Edward I. It is probably one of the most spectacular of the castles in north Wales. There are a lot of castles. But these are designated world heritage sites. Famous for its seven-year siege in the 1400s, it inspired the famous welsh song Men of Harlech and is now open to the public.

On my first visit, I made two major mistakes. The first was not realising that to visit the castle you had to make a booking. This was a bit frustrating and meant having to come back another day. This wasn't so bad for me as I did so after visiting Criceth, Porthmadog and Pwllheli. The second biggest mistake was deciding to carry on down the hill and having a little nose. Coming back out of the side road, I made the silly mistake of reversing back in front of the castle. Before I knew it, I had got too far into the hill before driving forward and risking burning the clutch out. I had managed to put myself on the steepest hill in England and Wales. Not knowing what else to do, and with a sense of panic, I hoped for the best and reversed all the way down to the bottom, getting some strange looks as I did so. I won't make that mistake again.

Porthmadog was an interesting town bustling and not camper van friendly, so I made my way along to Cricieth, where I pulled in to a parking space along the seafront road just in front of the castle itself, which again was closed. Low season see. after a night spent in one of the few pubs in what seemed like a very depressing town, I headed off the next morning to Pwllheli.

Pwllheli is famous for its Butlins holiday camp, so I thought there might be a bit of life in the town. Low season as it was, I was wrong. Pulling into the main car park in the centre square of the town, I sat and looked around for a bit before deciding to get some very nice fish-n-chips. Pointing to my motorhome and asking the staff, I was told it was fine to park there overnight and no one would bother me. After eating my meal, I had a nap before heading out and around the pubs set around the square. Before doing so, I went into the local supermarket to get myself a bottle of wine for later and was impressed to see live lobsters in a small aquarium being sold. Very unusual, I thought.

Calling into the pubs, I felt an immediate sense of depression at the mundane attitude of the locals sitting there, supping their pints, not even glimpsing up as I entered the bar. The women with their halves looking like the end of the world was nigh. Was it like this in the pubs around Birmingham or Sutton? I wondered. I'd never seen such miserable people. Not a smile amongst the lot of them. Butlins must be closed, I thought. No holidaymakers to liven the place up. No jobs to put a few quid in their pockets, just a sense of feeling that these were all spending their dole money and passing the time. It was making me depressed just watching them all sitting there, looking glum at the floor. Even the barmaid had a face as long as Livery Street. After a couple of hours, I made my way to my motorhome and drank a bottle of wine before settling in for the night. If I hadn't, I might have cut my throat. Driving down to and around the pretty harbour and seafront, I could see plenty of places to stop overnight and explore the area, but the sullenness of the pub and town last night had just put me off.

Originally, when my wife and I first bought our motorhome, the plan was straightforward. To tour England in the summer months wherever the fancy took us, north, south, east or west, just for short meaningful breaks. In the winter, abroad. Again, anywhere the fancy took us. Europe is an enormous place. But over the years, our plans altered somewhat. Now, alone, I have altered it around a bit; I find it much more enjoyable and easier to explore and enjoy England in the low season. No crowds, no officials looking to pounce on you at the first opportunity, and the roads are not so packed. In Europe, with less density, fewer people per square mile, more sun and better seas, and more importantly, a more relaxed attitude to the motorhome owner. The downside, especially being alone, was the lack of company when it would have been nice enough in a pub or restaurant. Calling into the pub in Pwllheli brings it home to me.

PWLLHELI AND LLANDUDNO

From Pwllheli, I had decided to pop over to Anglesey. Technically, Anglesey is an island which, in truth, I would never have visited in any other circumstances than with a motorhome. Originally part of the land mass of Wales, it occurred to me it was very separate and different from Wales. Even the people I spoke to seemed less Welsh. Accessed from the 19th-century Menai Suspension Bridge and the rebuilt Britannia Bridge, it is known for its beaches and ancient sites, the medieval town of Beaumaris and its 13th-century Beaumaris Castle with its concentric fortifications and a moat. Beaumaris gaol has its Victorian punishment cells and the original tread wheel. (Both are now thankfully closed.) It also has lots of blue flag beaches with varied coastlines, the fifth largest island in Britain. It covers 276 square miles and is separated by the Menai Strait. The island appeals to all the senses, a place to see and explore. Prince William lived on the island during his royal air force service, the first member of the royal family since Henry VII to do so.

My plan was simple, driving, stopping and visiting places as the fancy took me. A tour of the island would take about half a day, being only 75 miles around. First heading to Red Wharf Bay, I pulled into one of the quiet coves for the night with a choice between the beachfront, road, or car park. I chose the car park, toilets directly behind, and a bar and restaurant on the seafront. A small shop at the head of the sea road was selling freshly prepared crab, and directly opposite was the spa supermarket where I brought a loaf of crusty bread. I sat down to enjoy a nice evening snack overlooking the surf. Bliss!

I drove into a few of the bays in my tour of the island, from Red Wharf to Bull Bay, where I encountered a lovely group of ladies taking a morning dip in the freezing sea. A desolate boarded-up hotel was a sign of how bad things can get for the hotelier or businessman. With no one about, I was surprised to see a lady at the roadside selling ice cream and coffee. After a friendly chat, she informed me she opened up as often as she could. Her English was very good without a hint of welsh, yet the welsh language was taught and spoken by more than half the island.

Seeing a small sign saying exhausts, I took a chance and enquired. I had tried one or two garages around Birmingham to get a new exhaust fitted with little success. (Oh, how I miss my old pal, Bernard Haywood, the exhaust manufacturer.) Driving along a bumpy, muddy track that opened up to a large workshop, I asked the two guys if they had a new exhaust for my fiat Ducati. I nearly fell back when they told me they had indeed got a new exhaust and quoted me a price for fitting cheaper than I had been quoted in the big city. Without further ado, the younger guy got under my camper, got the old exhaust off, and replaced it with the new one, asking me to check as proof. After driving around for a few more hours, I spent one more night before heading off back to the mainland.

Llandudno, or 'Clandudno' as the welsh pronounce it (to confuse us, see), was only some 30 miles away and along the coast. With its north shore beach and 19th-century pier, the first time I visited was a bit of a revelation. Having been in the hotel business in north Devon, we were used to seeing rundown resorts. From the big hay days of the 50s and 60s, overtaken by Spain and its exotic resorts like Benidorm and

Lloret de Mar, golden beaches and warm blue seas, the British hotel didn't have much of a chance. Butlins, with its regimental 'hi de hi' mentality, wasn't far behind.

Places like Rhyl and Blackpool, with too many hotels and guest houses, were left well behind. Worse, with the motorway network, it was far easier to get to Blackpool within an hour from Birmingham, less from Manchester or Liverpool. People could drive up with their families and have a day out without the expense of accommodation. It didn't help that you could go to Spain for a fortnight, for less than a week in England, including flights. Llandudno was a bit of an exception. With its long promenade and fine sandy beach, it was a throwback to the Victorian era with all the modernity of modern hotels. Walking along the seafront, it wasn't hard to imagine yourself back in that time. With its splendid, well-maintained seafront hotels, attractive, bustling shops, cafes and restaurants, it was a pleasure to walk around and investigate. The cliffs of Great Orme jutted out into the sea, and ancient tunnels led to a cavern at great Orme mines. A 1902 tramway has an upper and lower section and travels to the summit of the headland to the east. Little Orme is a nature reserve. The award-winning north and west shore beach boast stunning views overlooking the Irish sea.

The 19th-century pier was a delight to walk along, with its variety of shops, cafes and amusements. You almost expected to bump into Victorian ladies and gentlemen walking along under their parasols. My only minor disappointment was the remark by the owner of the fresh seafood stall. I had a nice breakfast at one of the many cafes in the town, which was a bit at the higher end of the price. Now I had just paid him a rather, I thought, high price for some whelks and cockles. When I commented on the high price increases, he pointed out that one of his friends was a councillor in Llandudno and had told him that motorhome owners were not wanted in the town because we never spent money. Banter or not, I found it offensive, considering I had spent upwards of 17 quid, and it wasn't yet 12pm. Is this how some towns thought of us as campers? At any rate, I didn't reorder the same amount of seafood that I had intended. I don't think many others did either, judging by the lack of a queue.

Still, it didn't put me off enjoying the town's beauty or facilities. Getting on the open-top bus, I had a drive around the town to get a better viewpoint of the layout. Not only did the bus drive around the town itself, but it also took me down to Conwy, known to us English as Conway, a fascinating walled market town. The walled town and castle stand on the west bank of the river Conwy facing Deganwy on the east bank.

Conwy is a beautiful town, with small narrow streets that hold a variety of small shops leading down to the small harbour, all dominated by the imposing Conwy Castle. Known as one of the most magnificent medieval fortifications in Europe, built by Edward 1st during his conquest of North Wales circa 1282, it is also one of the best-preserved castles in Wales. Unbelievable as it may seem, there are over 600 castles in Wales, with a country so small you would expect to bump into a castle on every corner. When the expression was used that a man's home was his castle, they must have been referring to the welsh. The fee to go inside is not that expensive, though I feel and wonder how much better it would be if they adopted the attitude of the French with the medieval town of Carcassonne? Far from charging a fee, the castle and town made its money from public visiting and spending money in the many restaurants and shops.

Aston Hall was another fine example of not using its full potential. Yes, it held events, even midnight ghost hunting sessions, yet its grounds were mostly empty and under-used.

The entrance fees were not stiff, but with the Aston Villa Football Club directly opposite, what an opportunity to use the grounds to gain more income, especially in the summer months with mini fairs, tombolas, food stalls, etc. Oh well.

The extra benefit of sitting on the top open deck of the bus was it enabled me to view potential places to park my motorhome for overnight stays. On the other side of the great Orme, I could see one or two attractive places to park with a couple of campers already in place. Conwy was a different matter, small and enclosed by the castle walls. Narrow streets made it virtually impossible to park my motorhome for a couple of hours, never mind overnight. I had decided that to explore the castle, I would have to park well away and get the bus into Conwy itself. Fine; it was well worth the visit.

During my first visit to Llandudno, I parked up on the seafront road directly opposite the hotels that were closed. Another camper had the same idea further down. The sign displayed free overnight parking, which was all the encouragement I needed. Over two nights, I was not bothered. Two years later, the sign had changed, no overnight parking for campers. This time I had parked alongside the church in the centre of town, which displayed free overnight parking. Some campers parked overnight in the parking area for the train station. Other than that, there were various spots around the far side of the great Orme or along the seafront on that side. Once again, I found it frustrating that so many councils were not waking up to the growing number of fully self-contained motorhome owners. I am not talking about the small vans or conversions with no facilities, great as they are, but the fact that they do not have a toilet, for instance, creates its own problems, especially with children. In Barmouth, they have a car park over a quarter of a mile in length, empty for eleven months of the year. How stupid is that? For the sake of two or three grand, it could put waste tipping facilities and a cold water tap encouraging motorhome owners. How much would that further benefit the town?

Llandudno is a big town with, I'm sure, plenty of spaces that could be set aside just for campers. This argument that campers do not spend money is nonsense. Even a couple of pints in the local pub are better than nothing. Yes, we might want to cook our own food, but we have to buy ingredients and food from the local supermarkets. Sometimes I think these seaside councils deserve to suffer. Like many others, I don't wish to sound like a cheapskate. In business for most of my life, I can quite afford to pay for a site, but what am I paying for? The ability to sit on a patch of grass and put my table and chairs out? OK, it's convenient to have the toilet and shower facilities, but that's about all. I have a shower and a toilet, which is perfectly adequate for the two or three-day break I take, even with my kids. I have a 100-watt solar panel on my roof that keeps my batteries topped up, yet I'm made to feel a cheapskate because I don't want to waste 20 or 30 quid plus a night on something I don't need.

Why does Europe, France in particular, have such a different attitude? Yes, there are campsites, but you can't go five miles without coming across an Aire on motorways, villages and towns. The attitude is totally different; I have stopped in Aires in some glorious positions, like on the banks of the river Mayenne in Château-Gontier. In Martinet, Spain, by the French border just a few miles from Andorra, the Aires are in a fantastic position just across the bridge, yards away from the town centre. Amazing views across the mountains, toilets, waste tipping facilities and water, free and for small fee showers and electricity. The logic is by it being free, the campers will spend the money saved in or around the town. It doesn't take a lot of brains, does it. Each time I call into the site, which I often do, as I like it so much, there are at least ten motorhomes on it. If each of us spends twenty euros per night per van, that's a minimum of 200 euros a night, 1400 euros a week. I don't think that's peanuts. Sometimes I've seen as many as 40 campers, and like me, I've seen a few around the town in the restaurants or shops and bars. That costs the town nothing except a bit of land. I have seen this replicated all over France. A small profit may be made on the electric or showers, but it at least covers some of the cost.

A new or more recent phenomenon is the overnight pub park-up. Years ago, no respectable country boozer would allow you to camp overnight in their car park. Heaven forbid you even asked. Anyway, the campsites were cheap enough. Then slowly, things changed. Campsite fees climbed up as pub takings took a dive. Now every pub with a bit of land is scrambling at the gates offering free overnight parking if you buy a few drinks or a meal, of course, which is fine if you want a meal or a drink. If you don't, you ain't welcome.

Bet and I had our first experience when we called into a country pub in Snake Pass in the Derby Dales. We'd had a lovely couple of days hiking across the hills and were looking for somewhere to camp up for the night before heading off somewhere else when we noticed the pub. Pulling onto the vast car park, I called into the pub and asked the very nice landlady if we could spend the night in her car park as we wanted to have a drink and a meal. Pointing to the far end of the car park, she welcomed us to stay, advising us to use the far corner out of the way of her regular customers and guests because she also had letting rooms. Once inside, we ordered a couple of drinks and cuddled up to the fire, nice and cosy, whilst looking at the menu. Whilst making our choice, the landlady came over and introduced herself, took our order and sat down for a chat. Her husband was a farmer, and they had bought the pub on her recommendation to supplement the income from the farm. Having made an enormous mistake a few short years earlier by persuading my wife what a brilliant idea it would be to buy a country pub in Hereford, I commiserated with her about what a tough life running a pub was. Not the actual running of the pub, I might add. Oh no. It was dealing with all the local dickheads.

The problem with a country pub, be it in Wales or Hereford, is you are dictated to by the locals and boy, do they have the whip hand over you. Within two months of buying our pub, a beautiful traditional black and white, with five acres leading down to the River Wye, I knew I had made a serious mistake. The agents burst out laughing when I rang, but thankfully got a buyer for us straight away. Mentioning this to the landlady, she gave a weary sigh and admitted that the same threats had been made to her, even though her husband was a local farmer who's family had been here for generations. Kiss our backside, or we won't come back. Thankfully, she had a good tourist and food trade, so she made it very clear where the door was. She never got threatened again.

The food was standard pub food, adequate, but nothing special. Whilst we'd got a couple of nice chicken legs, we decided we could have them the next night somewhere else. As it turned out, a lovely little field next to a stream with a lovely mountain walk just a quarter of a mile further down the hill. We enjoyed the meal and the drink, and it was what we both wanted to do, fortunately, but it also made us aware that it could become an expensive habit if we did this regularly. By parking in the pub car park, we had saved on camping fees, of course, but the meal and the drinks turned out to be far more expensive than a campsite and without the electricity. Now, more and more pubs are offering this facility for having a meal and/or at least a drink or two. The problem is, where do you draw the line? A pint is now quite expensive. It seems mean-hearted to question these things, but if you intend to spend a lot of time camping or travelling, then you have to think about it.

When we bought the pub in Hereford, specifically for its camping potential, it was a member of the caravan and camping club CLs that gave us permission to have up to five vans at £6 a night. 6 quid a night? With an electric hookup, it was ridiculous. Worse, none of the campers spent a bean in the pub. They were using more electricity. Those camping clubs are not slow, are they? My suggestion would be for any pub to charge a one-off straight fee of circa £6 without electric hook-up for, say, a maximum of three or even two nights. That way, the choice is yours whether to have a drink, to have a meal or not, with no pressure on either party. The problem is even this can become a bit of a grey area. On some motorhome sites, I'm seeing more and more pubs putting themselves up for letting. Even farmers with a muddy field put out feelers to the camping community, who then suggest a price of ten or fifteen pounds. Then some dimwit will poke up and say, "Oh yes, that's a fair price. I would certainly pay for that." Well, of course, you might, Petal Dove, for the one night in the year that you come out. But a muddy field ain't worth fifteen quid.

I have one or more pubs that I enjoy going to as a destination pub for a night or two. Just a couple of miles outside Stourport is a lovely little hamlet called Pensax, with only one bell pub. There is a small car park opposite the pub but also a lovely, well-kept CL, run by a lovely farmer named Andrew. I often pop over, just for a night or two, to enjoy the ambience of the pub and the locals. Regularly, they have a group of musicians doing a jamming session. Absolutely delightful.

Another little favourite is the Crown at Calcott Bridgewater, Somerset. Very popular with the locals and motorhome owners, it has an extensive car park, regular entertainment and good food. Ok, it's a bit of a run from Sutton Coldfield, but I spend at least two or three nights there over New Year's Eve. Well, sometimes you have to push the boat out. But there are lots of little gems like this around the country. We each have to find our own.

I have a neighbour who lives in a very nice corner four-bedroomed detached house in Sutton, with a swimming pool, I might add, who has two golden rules. One, he will let no one near his motorhome indoor toilet. That is a definite no, no. Which I happen to go along with fully, as do most motorhome owners. Rule two is he just won't pay to go on a site. Having had his motorhome for many years, he has just built up a natural aversion to paying to go on a site, once telling me he even parked up once on someone's drive. That, to me, is taking the biscuit, yet he even appears on television programmes. But this is the beauty of the motorhome. It's the feeling of complete freedom that comes with it. I have been to many a hotel holding a boxing competition that I attend regularly or some other event in my motorhome, and I parked up for the night in the car park. One year, I booked into the Grosvenor hotel in Skegness for the Christmas period. The hotel was owned by a very nice cockney guy who made us feel very welcome. Another bonus, an old friend, John Lodge, was the entertainer. Booking in for the Christmas Eve and Christmas Day dinner, I parked in the parking bays on the quiet side road adjoining the hotel. Nice and peaceful. Who is going to object over Christmas? It was a great occasion, made even nicer that we shared a table with the host, who kept the bottles of wine flowing liberally throughout.

LONGER BREAKS ABROAD

The actual difference in attitudes only hits you when you get abroad, onto that little ferry to Calais or Santander. Ok, we know both countries are twice the size of England, but England holds circa 70 million people (that's what we're told. Lord knows how many illegals are in the country.) France holds circa 60 million, with Spain even bigger, holding some 40 million. Imagine driving around England with its true capacity of some 40 million people. We all sit back like dummies accepting this difference, without saying a word for fear of being called racist by those few, for reasons of their own, who think it's all great. Mainly, I suspect, from that one per cent at the top of the tree, which are surrounded by acres of land and a villa somewhere nice that they can escape to when it suits. This is how it has always been and will continue to be. It's all about money. You see, more people bring in more money. More money means more taxes. Simple *ay*?

Getting off the ferry at Calais and once out of the city limits, the landscape changes visibly. Outside the normal rush hour traffic periods, the roads can be almost empty. Mile after mile of straight Romanesque tree-lined roads open out before you. If you drive on non-toll motorways, you can relax without feeling you are on a rat run. For perfect peace, the toll roads and village roads are even quieter. Like most people who first set off abroad, we were terrified, Bet more so. Right-hand side driving to boot. First, Bet couldn't read a map to save her life, bless her heart. It led to countless arguments and many stops where I had to read the map and then chug along before stopping again. It was bad enough in England. The thought of driving abroad was horrendous. But by the time we had got our motorhome, some bright spark had come out with the invention of the sat nav, literally worth its weight in gold. I tell you, you don't know what driving is till you've got the sat nav.

Getting off the ferry, I would simply type in Benidorm for Spain or Cannes for France. Bet would sit back and enjoy the ride. I could relax in comfort, knowing we were going to get there. Even better, every time we pulled off the road and restarted, a little voice would pop up saying, please drive on the right, a godsend. All of this was the first bonus.

In England, we have been brainwashed for years, don't go to France with those froggies; they hate us anyway. On every street corner, the French police are waiting to jump onto any English number plate and hammer us with expensive fines. England is the best and finest country in the world, the best place to work and live, and the best place to own a home. All nonsense, of course. Well, I'd agree if it wasn't so packed. The second most important thing we notice is the relaxed, even accepting attitude toward the motor homer. The first thing is the motorways. You won't go more than five miles without seeing a sign for an Aire. These are literally what they say. Aires, spaces that you can pull into and relax. Car lorry or camper van, there is no discrimination. Some are isolated and quiet, others are busy and adjoining motorway services.

Being used to the English way of doing things, it takes a bit of getting used to knowing that you can pull in, park up, have a meal and tuck in for the night without some official screaming at you to move on or slamming a ticket on your windscreen. Is it that age-old sickness that besets the British? Us English. Jealousy. We are known for building someone up and then knocking them down when they finally get to the top of the tree. We see it regularly amongst pop stars or people who are successful in or out of their field. How many times and examples do we see this in the newspapers? At the first opportunity or chink in the glass, we are in there like a shot, all guns firing, ready to claw them back down with a vengeance. Motorhomes are a perfect example. I never gave much thought to it until I spent more time abroad. Pull up somewhere in England, and you might get the odd look. I initially thought it was admiration. Pull up in what is perceived to be the wrong spot or place, and you get a dirty look.

Do the same in France, Spain, and most other European countries, and no one notices you. You're of little consequence. You're just another motorhome, another visitor. Growing up as I did in the inner city of Birmingham, I saw this attitude grow as people progressed and finances improved. Anthonys, who owned the corner shop on the road where we lived, had bought a nice brand new Zephyr car. No one envied the shop owner. We all knew the couple worked hard, but as the country progressed, things picked up financially, and attitudes started to change. Imperceptible at first, jealousy or resentment would never be admitted to. No, it was more a dislike. That's different. 'Oh, her, Mrs Dainty Two-Shoes', or, 'Oh him, he's a right pillock he is'. Initially, I remember going along with it, thinking he must be a pillock because someone said so. It was only as I got older that I started to question it. Very often, it was through some resentment or petty jealousy.

I've seen it on campsites by some van owners towards other van owners. I've seen it towards older camper vans and their owners. Quite pathetic, really, and totally unnecessary. In Europe, I've seen some right contraptions, home-made tongue-and-groove jobs on the back of pickup trucks. I've had one-tonne vans pull up alongside us in Morocco with DC transport Denmark on the side, tables and chairs pulled out, and beds folded up.

In France and Spain, homemade van conversions and horsebox conversions are stacked with solar panels on the roof. In the Pyrenees, a lady came over to say hello. She then proceeded to pop up her tent on top of her car, step ladders out of her estate to climb up, and she was over sixty. Marvellous. Most times, I could only stop and wonder in admiration for their ingenuity. Especially for the home made conversions. Look, no one is better than the next man. Some are just more fortunate or luckier than others. No matter where I've parked up in Europe with consideration, of course, most people don't even look up or seem to notice. I've pulled into village car parks, town car parks and out-of-the-way town squares. Driving out of a Carrefour supermarket one late afternoon, I noticed a large space on the other side of the river with a few lorries in. Pulling in and heading to the far side, I settled down for the night, only realising that there was an Aires adjoining the supermarket with other campers in.

Driving along late one night, it was getting darker and darker. Some places I passed that were suitable, I carried on, thinking something more suitable might come along. Eventually, I entered a small village with a restaurant to the side that was obviously closed. Turning around, I pulled into the car park, settled myself in, and put the kettle on. Within the hour, I noticed another motorhome slow down and pull in. French, ahh, it must be alright then. Relaxed, I got into bed. The next morning whilst drinking my coffee and looking at the old houses across the road, I noticed an old lady walk out, potter around for a good twenty minutes and in all that time, she never even looked across. If she did, it was discreet. This was the France I was beginning to see and enjoy, chilled, relaxed, and easygoing.

Naturally, in built-up areas, it is different. Not everywhere is the same. In Carcassonne, for instance, the medieval city, there is a designated campervan parking area set aside on the far side of the parking area where you can spend the night for a small fee. Many, if not most, places provide free parking around the country. Vineyards, wine producers, cheese makers. In Lagrasse, the medieval village with the St Marie Monastery, there is an olive grove to the side of the village, exclusively for campervans. For me, that alone is worth the visit. The village itself is delightful, with interesting narrow streets and houses, restaurants, and a couple of taverns. Surprise, surprise, a Michelin-starred restaurant.

In a small seaside resort in Viareggio, Italy, some four miles from the birthplace of Puccini, and where he wrote most of his operas, I called in to spend a few days. Quickly I found myself a nice little spot on the seafront road minutes from the beach. Pulling into the corner, I opened the door, settled down and put the kettle on, a common ritual. Sitting on the sofa, I felt a little dog walk past my door, and then he came past again, grunted and carried on past. Grunted? A dog. I got out and looked outside, puzzled. I realised it was a baby boar, a wild boar, then another, then its mother, then its father. Before long, there were about 8 of them. The locals turned up most nights at around 7pm to feed them. They just came out of the forest behind me. It was marvellous, absolutely exhilarating, and no one paid a blind bit of attention to little old me sitting there taking it all in. I wondered if there was an ulterior motive. Nice whole fresh wild boar.

THE EAST COAST OF ENGLAND

I have to confess I'm not a great fan of the east coast. I mean, no offence to people living in the east, but, well, the sea is so uninviting; the land is flat and uninteresting. I once worked around the coast of Skegness and Ingoldmells. Great being young and working there. Not so great for holidays. I know because I used to hear the moans of the holidaymakers. Someone with great imagination and a flair for the dramatic came up with the idea of the cheerful blustering sailor and the catchy slogan 'Bracing Skegness' or 'Blustering Skegness', probably Billy Butlin, followed by 'wish you were here', both of which I'd rather forget.

One of my more unpleasant brothers-in-law, a ginger nut named Clive, had won a competition in the comedy section. Apparently, his cousin was a professional comedian. I'd never heard of him, but Clive thought he could emulate him and be a professional comedian himself. He'd won a competition at one of the Butlins camps and got through to the semi-finals at Caister: you have to take your hat off to Butlin. What a clever bloke. I worked at Butlins, and he had every aspect covered. The red coats were would-be entertainers, paid not much more than the rest of the staff, but the redcoats and the cache of being an entertainer, it boosted their ego. The other great gimmick was the competitions, the 'knobbly knees' competition, the 'glamorous granny' competition, and the 'best singer' competition. And for some, it was a great platform. But for Billy, and ensured his camps filled up in the low season when otherwise they would be empty. As a morale booster, Clive and his wife Pauline asked us to go along for a bit of moral support. We were pleased to do so. That's what families do, after all.

First, Clive's accommodation was free as part of his winning the competition. The only problem was that Clive's accommodation was only suitable for one; himself. Naturally, he'd had to pay for an upgrade for his wife and children individually. Then, of course, we had to pay for ourselves. That was just our party. Some would-be contenders were lucky enough to bring an army of relatives. No one knew who was who. When a roar went up for a comedian, it not only helped the comic's confidence, it also helped sway the judges. The very shrewd comics or entertainers spread their families around the other few holidaymakers in the audience. When the roar went up, everyone felt that it was the best act of the night, even though a few thought it wasn't. Sadly, it didn't do a lot for Clive's confidence. With an allocated two or three-minute slot, Clive lost it in the first thirty seconds and froze. It was awful. We just didn't know what to say or do. Poor Clive lost.

We made the rest of our holiday in Caister, but it wasn't through Clive that we just didn't enjoy the holiday. Caister is one of those holiday towns that were great in the 60s before Spain was discovered, like Great Yarmouth, Skegness and Blackpool, bumper cars, ghost trains and big dippers, strong blustery, chilly winds, and murky brown seas. A more telling indictment was on a Saturday morning, leaving day. It was like clocking off time at one of the big major car factories. The holiday camp had to be vacated by 12pm, at 10am, before even breakfast, the last free meal, and the car park was like a racetrack with everyone trying to escape. Caister has shops, Caister Castle, more shops, and the famous four-mile walk to Great Yarmouth, and that's about it. As soon as that ding dong went, followed by 'morning campers. Hi, de, hi', everyone was off,

Further north and to Skegness, you have the Wash and Boston. The Wash is an open stretch of sea that is deemed too dangerous for swimming. Boston, at one time, was a beautiful market town renown historically for its markets and fresh fruit, vegetables and flowers from around the local farms established some 450 years ago. The market sits alongside St Botolph Church, known and famous as the Boston stump. Boston had a heritage all of its own. People, locals, had been born and bred there for centuries, rarely leaving the close-knit community. But slowly, the physical landscape started to change. The local farmers and fruit and veg growers, desperate to keep the wages low, started importing Polish workers who were equally desperate for better-paid work. Initially, the idea worked very well; the Polish were a respectable and polite race of people. The local farmers and crop growers even put caravans on site for the workers who would arrive en masse, and spend the summer picking fruit and vegetables, saving their earnings to send back to their families. It was a great arrangement that suited everyone, the locals who didn't want the work, the farmers, the supermarkets, and the Polish people themselves.

Then the government changed the goal posts by agreeing to join the common market in 1972, which eventually led to the Polish people being able to live here permanently. Now, they didn't have to leave at the end of the season. Even better, they could claim all the benefits available, rent, rates, child benefits and so on, which obviously were a great deal more than they were eligible for back in Poland. For the poles, it was fantastic. They were getting more child benefits here than the average wage back in Poland. No wonder they didn't want to go back home. But the problem was, it led to boredom. From being decent, hardworking people, they descended into drinking and hanging about the town. Worse was to follow.

The Bulgarians were then applying to join the European community. As such, they were entitled to come here and also work at cheaper rates than the poles. Those Lincolnshire farmers are nothing if not slow. For a few shillings fewer, they could get swathes of Bulgarians coming over, working even harder and cheaper than the poles. Now Boston is rated as one of the worst and most dangerous towns in Britain. Groups of Bulgarians and Polish hang around the town, getting drunk, urinating wherever they congregate and fighting. Now, sadly, from being a peaceful, beautiful market town, it has descended into a dangerous and unpleasant place to live. Once upon a time, it used to be a nice, interesting place to visit, even to stay in the motorhome. But not now. I just wonder how those farmers feel and if they have any guilt for the local community that they have helped kill off. Of course, they themselves live outside of the town. Their children also, probably in many cases, go to private school, and if one bad thing happens, well, it's not their fault, is it? Great *ay*.

What about the government? Do they give any thoughts or concerns for the public, the great unwashed, us? Immigration is changing the entire face of society in our country, and no one is giving a damn about it. Some towns and cities are outnumbered by the immigrant population, and if we say anything about it, we're told to shut it and stop being racist.

SKEGNESS AND
THE EAST COAST

Skegness lies just a few miles northeast of Boston. Originally a Roman site on the side of The Wash known as the Ness, it gained fame in the early 1900s when the British public knew no better and some clever clogs came up with the slogan 'Skegness is so bracing' and a picture of a jolly fisherman, 'ho, ho, ho,' for the newly arrived British Railways. Well, they'd got to get you there and buy a train ticket. Billy Butlin did the rest, with a few quid in his bin and the bluster of the showman. He leased a chunk of land just north of Skegness itself from the Earl of Scarborough in 1927. The land had originally been an early RAF base in the First World War, with all the huts still in place. Where others saw a major and costly burden, Billy saw an opportunity.

For very little money, Billy set up stalls and entertainment during a time of dire austerity to give the British public a cheap and entertaining holiday. Born in Canada to a fairground family, he came to Britain and eventually started off owning and running his own stalls. From opening his first camp in 'Skeggy', Billy then opened his second camp two years later in Clacton. During WW2, and seeing another opportunity, he leased his first two campsites to the government before buying them back at the end of the war. The man was a ruthless genius with the fairground in his blood. Interestingly, it was said that the man was so ruthless and had so many enemies that he carried a cut-throat razor in his pocket at all times for protection. Those fairground guys just never change, do they? From establishing his holiday camp in Skegness, he opened the doors to many others who jumped onto his shirt tails, opening pubs, restaurants and caravan sites stretching from Skegness to Ingoldmells further along. Today, in many respects, Skegness is one big holiday camp, sadly struggling to survive. At one stage, it was easy enough to find somewhere to park up in your motorhome, in the town itself, or even in the car park of the Derbyshire miners club. Today it's more difficult. Every square site big enough for a caravan pitch has been taken up.

Many years ago and in my youth, I got chatting with my mate Dodger, who was leaving the next day to get a job at Butlins Skegness. Would I like to go along with him? This was a time when you could walk out of a job at twelve o'clock and into another at 1pm (yes, hard to believe now.) Being out of work and with nothing better to do, I agreed to go with him. With very little money, we hitched it all the way from inner city Birmingham to Skegness. Until that time, I had never ventured out of the city except for the odd school charabanc trip to the Cotswolds or Weston-super-mare. But Dodger, a year older than me, was a more seasoned traveller. What I didn't realise at the time was Dodger was also workshy.

It was the norm for many people to just pull into Butlins at the gates and ask for a job. Dodger, having worked there before, knew the score, knowing some people there. In particular, the cook with whom he blagged himself a job as a second chef. I got in as a dishwasher. Allocated a chalet with two bunk beds, we set too straight to work. For the first week, it was an adventure just getting to know and familiarise me with the camp. The chalets were set out in groups of rows from one end of the camp. (Think of some of the German prison camps or RAF bases) In rows over two stories were the holidaymakers. At the bottom end of the camp, next to the sewage plant, were the camp workers, me and Dodger included. The camp could hold

2,000 holidaymakers, with two sittings inside three restaurants. There were three bars, including the posh gentleman's bar and the Pig and Whistle pub. Every Butlins camp was laid out in the same format as a Pig and Whistle pub in every camp.

Think about the shrewdness of the man. All this was back in the 1930s. Having already been running a fairground in the town, Billy wanted to draw more customers in. the campsite was a stroke of genius by basing all the campsites on the same format. It meant holidaymakers who went from one campsite in Skegness to another, say in Clacton, felt immediately at home. The Pig and Whistle could hold up to 1,000 people at a time and, with the big stage, was the main entertainment area. With an indoor and outside swimming pool, slides and a fairground, snack bars and restaurants, Butlins had everything the camper could ask for. Few wanted to venture outside the camp, which was exactly what Billy anticipated, spending all their money inside.

Another minor side effect that Billy expected was the sexual explosion that would be created by being in such heady proximity to one another, mixed with gaiety and drinking. This would bring in more and more people in the hope for and anticipation of more sex. It worked, and it was true, although I never realised this at the time. After a week of getting to know the place, making friends and settling down, I started feeling right at home. The first lesson we were all to learn was don't touch the local girls after the first month of the start of the season. After that, it was open season on the camp with lovely new fresh girls arriving every Saturday. Life was bliss.

After a couple of weeks, and because of my ability as a boxer, Dodger had put me up for part-time security around the bars with the head of security, Jock. For this, I was paid two pounds more a week for wearing an armband and patrolling the bars. Apart from being easy and enjoyable work, the bonus was the number of holiday-making girls who were curious enough to come over and ask us what we were doing, to which we replied, "security." The next question, with a knowing look, was, "did we protect their chalets?" By the end of the night, we would have a list on the back of our arms with a tick against the prettiest of the girls. Yes, heady times, alright. Thank you, Billy Butlin.

From Skeggy, the drive up north gets a bit more interesting. Still barren, cold and windswept, the land can be bleak and uninspiring. That jolly sailor from Skegness could have been bracing himself anywhere along that coastline. Just a few miles further along comes Mablethorpe, which is very popular with campers and static van owners. It is also famous for its seal sanctuary and sand racing. Yes, the sand is so flat along this stretch of the coast that they came up with the idea of holding regular races on it, helped with that bracing wind, of course, and a two-mile coastline.

The town council runs a weekly market, and it's a regular pleasant walk from Skegness along the seafront. To do and keep the kids interested, fun can be had at the Lincolnshire Aqua Park, with plenty of places around to park up for a night or two. But the seal sanctuary and wildlife centre make a great day out with plenty to see and do. Queens Park has a paddling pool and boating lake, mini golf, mini train and a large car park. Both were adequate to spend the night. There are plenty of spaces and places to spend the night. At Monks Bay, there is a model railway, the Mablethorpe fairground, also a small ceramics studio where the kids can learn how to make cups and other things.

Saltfleet, some six miles north of Mablethorpe, is another coastal town and holiday spot, again with a beautiful sandy beach and dunes. Thankfully, many of the attractions are undercover, smart thinking in view of the weather. Again, plenty of places to park up with the motorhome and explore the area. Not far is the Lincolnshire Wolds steam railway, with plenty of areas to park. Further along, heading north, is Grimsby. Grimsby is the north's biggest and most famous fishing town. The principal supplier of fresh fish to Birmingham and the midlands seafood markets. Standing on the banks of the river Humber and twinned with Cleethorpes, someone had a sense of humour when they named it Grim. It is, well, it was. Now it boasts a modern shopping centre. For years, Grimsby was a dying town, but the city council has started a regeneration scheme, including the Grimsby Heritage Trail, which stretches from the Kasbah, the historic port side area of smokehouses, shops and factories, to the city centre.

The port area of Grimsby is a rough area, with its hardy fishermen having to go out in all kinds of weather to earn a living. Many years ago, I had a friend who lived in Grimsby and worked on the fishing trawlers as his father had before him. Hardy and tough, he had coarse hands that looked like a pair of shovels. Shoulders hunched in a constant fisherman's stance. I never once saw him smile. *Eeeh*, it was grim in Grimsby, alright. He told me that in the good old days when the port was heaving with fishing boats, he could be away for a couple of weeks at a time, but after a good catch, they could earn thousands. Some tales he told me were hair-raising. Mountainous seas, sinking fishing boats, lives lost at sea. Having to cut up and gut fish whilst trying to keep your footings in heavy rolling seas? Back in port, they would head for the nearest pubs and throw money around like there was no tomorrow. Sadly, there wasn't, and for a lot of them, the jobs went along with the big paydays. Yet another price to pay for joining the European Economic Community. As we were told, maybe Grimsby was not the town for a day's visit. It's a place you live and work in or try to get out of.

Further along, is Skipsea and its award-winning Skipsea Beach. With a long narrow stretch of sand, holidaymakers go to Skipsea for peace and quiet and to get away from it all. Its only castle was destroyed in 1221 when Count William de Forz rebelled against the king. A hundred years later, it was leased for pasture. The nearest railway station is Bridlington, some ten miles away. Skipsea probably got its name from the Viking word for ship lake, likely because the original village was on a lake, but the north sea keeps making inroads into the clay cliffs at the rate of 18 inches a year. Soon there will be no Skipsea. The area is also known for its sudden mists, which can roll in off the sea and shroud the village. William the Conqueror gave the Isle of Holderness to one of his knights, who built a castle surrounded by earthworks at Skipsea Brough. The knight then killed his wife, who is said to haunt the district as the white lady. She probably comes in with the mist. He probably killed her out of sheer boredom. Other strange tales and legends have grown up around the town, such as the footprints in fields around the castle where two brothers fought a duel. Strangely, nothing grew there afterwards. Skipsea was once chosen in the fifties for nuclear testing, but after strong local protests, the idea was abandoned. Skipsea is a delightful village with a small community of around 600 people with its historic squat-towered church, All Saints. With two swimming pools and miles of walking and cycle routes, there is plenty to do. The village has a modern school, post office, café and fish-n-chip shop. The terraced houses and garden walls are built from the cobbles sourced along the beach many years ago.

Close to Skipsea is Flamborough Head, with the oldest surviving lighthouse in England, built circa 1674. This area is a breeding ground for gannets and puffins and has plenty of places to park up in your motorhome. Skipsea Castle, with its motte and bailey castle, can also be visited with its car park easily accessible and great views from the top of Skipsea Brough. The green motte was some 45 ft high and surrounded by eight acres of land once flooded as a marshy lake. With a small basket fire going from a bit of scavenged driftwood, we enjoyed a pleasant couple of nights there listening and watching the puffins and gannets fighting and singing.

In the east riding of Yorkshire, Flamborough sits on the famous promontory of Flamborough Head, famous for its lighthouse. The headlands extend some six miles into the north sea, with the chalk cliffs extending up to 400 feet. The Church of St Oswald's stands in the village and is a grade II listed building maintained by Historic England. The village itself contains several shops and pubs, with the Royal Dog and Duck being in Dog and Duck Square. You wouldn't know that, maybe. Once recorded as merely a fishing village, half of which comprised fishermen, eleven farmers, a blacksmith, grocers, carpenters, a stonemason, a flour dealer, a schoolteacher and a gentlewoman. According to legend, the village is haunted by a suicide victim known as Jenny Gallows, though we never saw her.

With its holiday camps and caravan park, Flamborough is a holiday destination during the summer months. And North Landing was used in the filming of Dad's Army, the beach was also used for the TV drama Victoria. We had no problem finding somewhere to park up and spend a few nights around the headland with a short walk into the village for some nice fish-n-chips and a pint. Just a few miles away, Bridlington is a beautiful and popular seaside town. There are some run-down areas because of businesses inevitably closing, but there is plenty to see and do. The Bridlington Spa, with its dance floor and theatre rooms, was built in the late 19th century. There is a lovely café along the seafront with enormous glass windows looking out to sea. Typically, there are plenty of amusement arcades and a ten-pin bowling alley. The Priory Church is a magnificent building, free to enter and well worth a visit. By North Beach, there is a fairground with a few rides, including a big wheel. The harbour is a great place to catch some big fish, and you don't need a licence. There are also two land trains to see more of the town.

We enjoyed the short pirate ship ride from the harbour, but there is also North Beach, which differs from South Beach, the latter being a lot sandier. Historically, Bridlington was an old pre-Roman harbour and together with its majestic cliffs rising from out of the sea makes for some incredible views. To be fair, I found Bridlington one of the best places for a break along the east Lincolnshire and Yorkshire coast. Dramatic is a bit of an understatement. We found the locals helpful, which was a bit of a change, pointing us in the right direction to park up for a couple of nights at the local pub car park or the church car park.

Between Bridlington and Scarborough lies Filey, North Yorkshire, with imposing cliffs and long sandy beaches, in 2002, won the Sunday Times Beach of the Year competition. Sadly, unless things drastically pick up, I don't think it will win too many more competitions. When we called in, many of the shops were closed up, shuttered and run down. Just another sad aspect of the British way of life. Now it had become only a day trip out, being accessible by train and bus or car from Bridlington and Scarborough. There was no problem finding somewhere to park up for the night. I think the locals were quite grateful to see someone. If you like nature trails, then there are plenty, with the Wolds Way trail being one of them. The Filey Dams nature reserve is another point of interest, but we gave it a miss.

ONWARDS AND UPWARDS, WELL, AT LEAST NORTH TO SCARBOROUGH

Whenever I think of or hear the name, Scarborough, I think of the song Scarborough Fair. We fell in love with Scarborough, which we found a busy, attractive resort with two bays with sandy beaches split by the headland bearing the twelfth-century Scarborough Castle, now just a crumbling ruin. The Victorian Central Tramway funicular train links the town centre with South Bay and its harbour. Originally the site of a bronze age village and a fourth-century Roman signalling tower, Scarborough became the first major holiday resort in England, from the old Norse name Skarthi, meaning fortified town. You can see why. Once a spa town, it is now known for its parks, theatres and gardens.

Our first-ever visit to Scarborough was by booking into a hotel for a change. Seeing an advertisement offering a special deal, we booked into the Grand Hotel. The Grand had once been a Butlins hotel, and we, or should I say I, just never did my homework. Butlins always based itself on being cheap and cheerful. The new owners carried on the philosophy. The Grand looked magnificent, an imposing building overlooking the shore and near the funicular railway. It should have been a great four-day break. It was awful. Run down and dirty, the place was a tip with so many complaints on Trip Adviser it's a wonder it never ran out of pages. The position of the room was great, directly overlooking the sea, but the room was shabby, the carpet ruffled.

Going down to the "restaurant" in the basement, things didn't improve. The food was awful. Even the breakfasts, which are one of the easiest meals to make and serve up, were dire. The bacon was hard from being cooked from frozen. The only thing adequate was the eggs. After the second day, we ate in our room, me going down and fetching the best of what we could eat, egg on toast, toast with butter, the staff sullen and unfriendly. We cut short our stay, put a letter of complaint into the box, refused to pay, and walked out. Obviously, they were used to it, but we never heard a word back from them. Why couldn't they just keep the place clean and employ a decent chef? The more we experienced situations like that, the more we appreciated our motorhome.

Iron age tools dating back to around 500 BC have been found on the rocky headland where Scarborough Castle now stands, demonstrating its antiquity. First invaded by the Romans after they left, the Anglo-Saxons were free to invade. Some four hundred years later, the Vikings came in. It was these that gave Scarborough its name, 'borough', deriving from the word 'borg', meaning stronghold. It is funny to think that two Viking brothers invaded and harried in Ireland, Wales, and England and established a stronghold called Scarborough on the east coast, known to his brother as 'hare lip', or in the Viking language Skarthi, meaning Skarthies Stronghold in Norse. In 1066, in the months before the battle of Hastings, the town was attacked by Herald, the King of Norway.

Scarborough Castle was built around 1130 by the Earl of Albemarle. Captured by Henry II, he rebuilt the keep, and the castle became a royal castle. It was captured a few times by different kings under different sieges, with different people being put in charge of protecting the castle over many hundreds of years. The last was the shelling of the castle by German bombers during WWII.

Henry III established a fair at Scarborough by charter, and it was held in the town until 1788. It is remembered by us all in that age-old song that we all remember.

> *'Are you going to Scarborough fair?*
> *Parsley, sage, rosemary, and thyme.*
> *Remember me to one who lived there.*
> *She once was a true love of mine.'*

All those years ago, and we still remember that song, yet few sing it today. Listen to Simon and Garfunkel singing it. It's easy to transport yourself back to that time and place.

The medieval town grew beneath the castle, with the old part of the town centred on streets such as East Borough Friar Gate and Toller Gate. Scarborough was developed as a holiday resort in 1620 when spa water was discovered by Ms Farrow, who claimed that the waters had healing properties. The gentry flocked to the town to sample the qualities of the water, and its development really took off with the arrival of the railways in the 1850s. We found the town a very enjoyable experience to walk around from the north shore to the harbour and beyond. The only disappointment I found was in the fish and chips and the price of the seafood. Look, we are on a major fishing port, just a few miles up from Grimsby. Why cheapskate on portions and sizes? In any fish and chip shop in Birmingham, you get a good-sized portion of cod and a lashing of chips. Now, here we are, going into a fish shop and ordering fish and chips, cod and chips, and getting a thin slither of cod fillet bulked up by the batter, put in an undersized container and served with a small portion of chips. Where is the thinking in that? Are you going to go back again every day for the same meal? The cockles, whelks and prawns are sold in small portions. The portions were smaller than those served in Birmingham Bulls Ring, yet they are transported from Grimsby. I'm right next to Grimsby. I went into the one chip shop and asked if I could pay extra for a piece of cod loin instead of a fillet.

Above Scarborough lay Robin Hood Bay and the famous Whitby, where Bram Stoker's Dracula landed. Bram Stoker was in Whitby on business, stopping at six Royal Crescent. He had a week on his own to explore before being joined by his wife and baby son. Each morning he would take a walk around the town, taking in views that had excited writers for over a hundred years. Whitby's windswept headlands, the dramatic abbey ruins and a church surrounded by sweeping bats, the mist rolling in all added to the atmosphere of the place. Whitby Abbey stood above Whitby, the ruin of a once great Benedictine Monastery, founded in the 11th century. The medieval monastery stands on the site of a much earlier monastery founded by an Anglian princess. Looking right over the town is the ruin of Whitby Abbey, which was raided by the Danes. Below the abbey stood St Marys Church, reached by climbing 199 steps. The weather gnawing at the graves as they teetered precariously over the cliff edge. Some headstones stood over empty graves, the bodies long lost on distant shores. Stoker even wrote down some names from the graves and used them in his novel for Dracula's first victims. All that was needed was a visit to the local public library where he discovered a book, published in 1820, about the experiences of a British consul who mentioned a 15th-century prince, called Vlad Tepes, said to have impaled his enemies on wooden stakes. He was known as Dracula, the son of a dragon. Bram Stokers' book was born.

On the sands below East Cliff years earlier, a shipwreck of a Russian ship called the Dmitri from Narva ran aground whilst carrying a cargo of silver sand. Stoker simply rearranged the names and circumstances. Stoker spent six years on his novel and another six years before it was published, but the name of his villain and some of the most dramatic backdrops were inspired by his week's holiday in Whitby.

Whitby is a beautiful seaside town split by the river Esk, rising high above and overlooking the north sea. It makes an inspiring sight. The Captain Cook museum is set in the house where he once lived. Whitby has become more popular because of its association with Bram Stoker's Dracula, but its steep hills and great shops make it a great place to visit. We stayed the night in the car park near the monastery, and I must confess we both had an uneasy night. Only one uneasy night at that. Robin Hood Bay is a delightful little fishing village in the North Yorkshire Moors National Park. I must admit, it is a fantastic place for kids and adults. Bet and I fell in love with it. Wondering through its narrow cobbled twisting streets and alleyways, it's easy to imagine what it must have been like hundreds of years ago with its sailors' smugglers and press gangs.

I shouldn't knock some of the east coasts. Each part has something to offer. Some of it is barren, but places like Scarborough, Whitby and Robin Hood Bay stand up against anywhere in the world. Without a doubt, there are some beautiful places in England. I try and want to see as many of them as possible, enjoy them, savour them. But when I go abroad, I am met with a totally different attitude than in so many places here in England.

THE SOUTH AND CORNWALL

The Cornish people are yet another who say they want us, but they don't. They insist they are not the least insular but proud of their county, Cornish ice cream, and pasties. So proud are they of it they have even patented it and registered themselves as the only makers of the Cornish pasty, giving it protected status. This means that only pasties made in Cornwall from a traditional recipe can be called Cornish pasties. Even the crimps in the pasty are numbered and protected. The idea is traditionally a handy ready-made meal for the miners and land workers in the fields, with no soap or water in the fields or mines. The miner could pull out his pasty, grab the crimped crust and eat it without having to get his dirty fingers on his pie. After he had finished, the crimp would be discarded and thrown away. One day in the future, archaeologists will discover discarded wedges of half-moon specimens and pronounce them a scientific discovery, like the sandals found in the pyramids.

I mean, think about it, the pasty has to be made to a specific recipe and can only be called a Cornish Pasty if it's made via that recipe and sold in Cornwall. The mind struggles to imagine all those hundreds of years ago when some Cornish miner's wife had the bright idea of first coming out with the pasty at her kitchen table for her dear husband, Enyon. "Here, Enyon, take this down with you, and make sure you hold the crust."

"What a brilliant idea," say all his workmates, telling their wives to do the same with a crimped edge containing numbered edges. Some would use a potato and peas recipe, some meat, others fish, but whoever came up with the idea in the first place? Who then came up with the idea that this only belonged to us Cornish people, don't share it. It seems odd to me. Who is to know a Yorkshire family of miners never took a few pasties down to Cornwall on holiday, and the Cornish housewife, being savvy, didn't nick the idea. A pasty is a pasty is a pasty. If it's made in a certain way, then quite rightly, it should be called a Cornish pasty, whether it's made in Cornwall or Doncaster. My mom invented the stew. Well, I believe she did. She told me so, but everyone boasts about my mom's stew but calls it their own, the cheek of it. So we have the English stew, Scottish stew and Irish stew. We don't hear too much about the Welsh stew.

In Wales, they boast about the Welsh breakfast, but the Welsh breakfasts I have seen have been the same as an English Sunday breakfast. On Sunday, we throw the lot in. If that isn't enough to tell you about the Cornish psyche, you only need to look at their obsession with keeping the Cornish language all to themselves. Then let's not forget the Cornish cream tea or scone. This can only be prepared in a certain manner. Crikey, there have even been fights about it. To confuse you even more, cream scones are a traditional Cornish and Devon speciality, but the word scone originated in Scotland, and scone comes from the Dutch word 'schoonbrot', which means beautiful bread. Now that throws the mix up a bit.

The Cornish clotted cream was registered as a protected designation of origin in 1998. The cream is skimmed off the fresh milk and scalded in trays to the desired consistency. Cornish clotted cream is protected under European and English law. The milk cream must originate in Cornwall. Worse, it has to be served in a specific way. The Cornish insists it has to be spread jam first on the scone with the clotted cream on top (or vice versa). The Devon clotted cream has to be spread clotted cream first with jam on top (or vice versa). Does it matter? I don't think there is anyone in the country, in the world perhaps, who doesn't love a clotted cream scone.

The very first time I went to Cornwall was when a kindly neighbour, for some strange reason, offered to take me with him and his wife. This was to Mousehole, some 240 miles away from the inner city of Birmingham. I was about 7 at the time, and I had to sit on the back of his bike whilst his wife sat undercover in the sidecar. With no motorways back then, nothing was spoken about for the entire drive except for a half-hour break in Bristol, when my kind benefactor pointed to the Clifton Suspension Bridge and informed me about the daredevil pilot who flew his plane under the bridge. I can never remember whether the pilot survived or died.

Cornwall, to me, Mousehole, in particular, was magical. The harbour, something I had never seen in my life, was a dream. We stayed two nights, with me sleeping at the bottom of the bed top-n-tail in between the two of them. I remember heady days playing in the sand and grubbing for god knows what. After an amazing holiday, we made our way back home again with me on the back of his bike, riding for hour after hour. In the teaming down nonstop rain and out of pity, a driver, seeing my plight, offered to take me the rest of the way in his car. It wasn't long after that I caught double pneumonia and was put into isolation at the Birmingham General Hospital, where I almost kicked the bucket and came out weighing less than half my weight and looking skin and bone. It must have been serious because I remember the priest standing over me. Being so young, it didn't stop me from enjoying the memory of my time in Cornwall, and I vowed that one day I would go back.

Cornwall is not somewhere you go to on a whim. It's a mission, an adventure that takes a lot of planning. The only problem was the first time, I didn't. In my usual cavalier way, I just told the kids we were going on holiday to Cornwall, and off we set in my one-tonne builder's van, air-conditioned with little rust holes throughout the floor. Fine in hot weather, horrendous in the cold. Two miles up the road to do a job was no problem. 250 miles along A and B roads to Cornwall was a nightmare.

Our first nightmare experience was the twisting country lanes. Narrow with high stone walls that you can't see over ten yards in front of. I was banging along at my usual speed, not giving much thought. Bet with her arm out of the open window when this juggernaut just shot out in front of me. Slamming on the breaks, s*****g myself and shouting to Bet to get her arms in at the top of my voice. All I could remember was the lorry driver's mouth muttering, 'no, no, no', whilst shaking his head from side to side. Miraculously, and how I don't know, I slowed down enough to let the monster drive past me without getting a scratch on the van and Bet's arm getting ripped to bits. We carried on the rest of the way at about 15MPH. You only need a couple of experiences to put you off someone or something for life. It wasn't exactly the height of the season, but heading into Mousehole, we found it was busy enough. I was still trying to pull myself together from the narrow escape. Cornish people must have been built tiny. The roads were narrow and winding for little people, crunched up tiny houses, leaning into and over each other. If you passed wind from the corner house, it felt like the entire community would know about it. Mousehole must have been called Mousehole for a good reason.

The traffic warden was the first one, growling and waving his arms in anger, like a windmill in a gale. I was about to turn right into a one-way street when he started bawling, 'No, no, no'. This way. Well, I'm a bloody tourist on holiday, ain't I? I don't know the roads. I'm a stranger. It didn't improve with the shopkeepers, sullen and ungrateful at receiving our money. Within about 40 minutes, I got the impression that these people, locals, felt they were doing us a big favour by allowing us into their little kingdom. This was the home of King Arthur and the round table, where all people were equal. I hadn't heard the word Grockle at that time. It was only many years later, when we bought a hotel in Devon that we came across the word. A very derogatory term for holidaymakers and tourists. Anyone living over 50 miles outside Cornwall or Devon is called a Grockle. They've probably got a protection order on that as well. I don't think I'm sensitive. Living in the middle of the country, I feel we have an even and well balance outlook. Northerners are known for their friendliness, and, on the whole, I've found it to be true. Yorkshire folk are blunt. Again, true. Londoners, well, I lived in London for 12 months in a place called Chiswick, a favoured place of the acting fraternity. Well, let's say London is known as one of the loneliest places in the country. With over four million people, many hardly know each other. I think it's got one of the highest suicide rates in the country. As for Hereford, well, don't get me started on that one.

For all that, Mousehole is a beautiful little place. The houses and shops rising above the harbour make for a lovely backdrop to your stay. The only drawback is the parking. This applies to many places in Cornwall, Falmouth and Helston and the south coast. So, you've not only got the unfriendliness of the locals towards us Grockles, but the sheer difficulty of getting there in your car. With a motorhome, it's nigh on impossible. The exception was the AFC, Mousehole, who let us stay in their car park for a small donation.

We found a completely different attitude in Gweek, where we visited the Gweek Seal Sanctuary. The seal sanctuary was set up in the early 1960s to save the many damaged, hurt, lost, and abandoned baby seals around the south coast. A guy named Ken Jones set up the sanctuary after finding a baby seal abandoned on the beach. As the numbers built up, he eventually set up and moved the site to where it is now. Set in some 42 acres on the lizard peninsular on the beautiful Helford Estuary, most of the sanctuary is set along one side of the site, so it was quite easy to walk around with nicely set out areas for sea lions, otters and goats. Dog friendly, there is a shop, play area and restaurant. It was Ken himself who picked us up at the time in a little mini train, picked us up from the car park and onto the site itself. Ken was a friendly and active guy who totally immersed himself in the sanctuary and every aspect of it. Modest as he was, he never introduced himself, and it was only one of his staff calling him by his name that we realised who he was. A charitable sanctuary, it seemed to have moved on over the years to become a little viable mini zoo. Open all year round except Christmas Day. The small, pretty village itself is worth a visit just to sample a snack or a meal, home to some 500 people.

Further nearby places of interest are the Flambard Village theme park in Helston, the Glendburgens Gardens in Helford and the Treban Gardens, 26 acres of beautifully laid out gardens leading down to the private beach at Helston. These places need at least half a day or more to fully enjoy and get the most out of them. For those who feel up to it and fit enough, the walk up to the Halliggye Fogou historical underground tunnels is well worth a visit. On the Lizard peninsula from the 5th century BC, these tunnels are an amazing sight to visit and explore. We sat down quite a few times just to rest and take it all in.

Mullion is the largest village in the peninsular. Together with its coves and rugged stretches of coastline, it is stunning with its white powder-soft beaches, the sea a beautiful turquoise. What a stark contrast to our views of the east coast of England, brown dirty, looking sea water which, having lived near to the sewage works at Butlin's holiday camp, always made me aware of what goes into it to give it its colour. The dramatic backcloth of the cliffs shaped by the Atlantic Ocean is breathtaking. Seafood restaurants abound, or you can take a picnic, as we did, along its coastal paths. Being out of season, we cheekily spent the night in the harbour after one local said we should be ok. Listening to the sea lapping at the harbour wall was bliss. As well as being the busiest, Mullion is also one of the most picturesque, with its assortment of shops, art galleries, pubs and tea rooms that sell amazing cream tea scones.

With Lands' End to the west and Falmouth to the east, Mullion is a great base to explore Cornwall from. Especially the 15th-century church of St Mellanus, with its richly carved oak benches and its biblical scenes, including Jonah and the whale. There is also an abundance of coastal walks and historical sites, including prehistoric burial mounds and Celtic crosses. We had a beautiful lobster meal in the thatched-roof Old Inn.

In the heart of the village, the Mounts Bay Inn was yet another atmospheric pub with a great menu. Owned by the national trust, Mullion Cove is a sandy beach which sits below the historic lifeboat station and the fully working Mullion Harbour, with a fishing fleet protected by the picturesque harbour. There is a small cave that we explored at low tide and was a handy hiding place for the pirates and smugglers of 100s of years ago. Further along, is Polurrian Cove, with yet another fantastic sandy beach. All along the coastline, there is an abundance of sandy beaches and beautiful coves, many of them owned and looked after by the national trust. Many little cafes sell fresh crab sandwiches or the traditional Cornish pasty. The Lizard Lighthouse is now open to the public after 250 years of guiding ships to safety. The National Trusts Poldhu Marconi Centre was closed when we visited, but this is where Marconi created the first transatlantic radio signal on the remote Cornish clifftops.

The really great thing about this far tip of Cornwall is its accessibility to so many places if you're touring in a motorhome. From Tintagel to Padstow, Bodmin Moor and Newquay on the west coast, to Helston is only a short 50-mile distance. We felt and found that we could see and experience many of the major places of interest around that area of Cornwall. Falmouth, Packet Quays and Pendennis Castle are just a quick hop away from each other. Falmouth is yet another beautiful little harbourside town. Following its steep walk down to the harbour, the third natural deepest harbour in the world, it hosts some of the biggest ships from around the world. In fairness, there is something for everyone in Falmouth, with little spots along the high street that show glimpses of the sea only meters away. With unspoilt creeks and secret coves along the Fai River, it has some of the best views in Cornwall. We spent three days on the castle beach cliff road. Not only was it quiet and out of the way, but it also had superb views across the bay and out to sea. Pendennis Castle had astounding views. A circular castle with its moat built by Henry VIII, leading onto Pendennis Point. There are tea shops, antiques, restaurants, famous names, historical battles, nautical tales, and secrets that abound here. The beaches are beautiful and amazing, with soft grainy sand. Take your pick from the Swanpool, Maenporth and Greenbank. With plenty of water sports, snorkelling, windsurfing or sailing, there is more than enough for everyone. Falmouth is also filled with plenty of gardens from prehistoric to prim and tidy, and not forgetting, the Eden project is just a short drive away. There is the national maritime museum set on the harbour, smuggling stories, and explorers all here. Why, it even has its own number one arts university with plenty to see. Very nice restaurants. We were never disappointed. The pavilion was a great place to see music and regular events, a jazz band playing whilst we were there. We climbed the 111 granite steps of Jacob's ladder, not the biblical one, well, downwards. It was built by a local businessman as a shortcut to his business.

From the edge of Falmouth, you can follow the beautiful and peaceful Helford River to Gweek, five miles away. With creeks leading off, the most famous being Frenchman's Creek, made famous by the Daphne du Maurier (novel of the same name), Helston is heavily wooded with lots of villages dotted around, all worth viewing. We viewed only half of them. Just across the water from Falmouth are St Mawes and the Roseland Peninsula. St Mawes, again, is an attractive harbourside village with steep cottages lining the streets. It's a bit upmarket and caters for this end of the market, with various royals having stopped here over the years and a bit of a magnet for celebrities. St Mawes Castle was built along with Pendennis Castle to defend the Fai River from the French invasion. Both castles are open to the public.

Another small tip for anyone travelling anywhere around the country. If you're looking for somewhere to pitch up for one, two or three nights, it's always worth looking up the local rugby or football clubs. Most medium-sized villages have a football club. Sometimes shared with rugby and cricket clubs. I've not met one yet who hasn't allowed me to park in their car park. Obviously, always be respectful, leave nothing but your footprints and offer to make a donation to their charity box. Most will refuse, but it's nice to make the offer. The other great thing about the clubs is the fact that no one else gets around them, so it's quite peaceful. For water, I haven't been to any fishing port or harbour that doesn't have a tap or water supply. Away from the sea, the cemetery is a good bet. Every cemetery has a water tap. In the country, out of desperation, I've often found a friendly farmer kind enough to let me fill up from his yard tap.

More of a problem, I find, is the waste disposal situation. My waste water tank holds 80 litres, and trust me, if you use it for all waste, it soon fills up. Washing up? 4—5 litres, three times a day. First, by using non-stick frying pans, we use paper to wipe the pan clean, with no water. Plates and cups, the same thing, followed up with a damp cloth. Unhygienic? Well, we've never had a problem. As for washing, well, a flannel does a good job, with a top n tail perfectly adequate. In our case, we have an outside shower, which is a bonus when needs must, especially on hot days coming off the sandy beach. If you cannot go a day or two without a shower or you feel the need to wash your plates and cutlery in a sink of hot water followed by clean running water, then you might be better off going to a campsite. Nice and roomy as your motorhome might be, it is not your home with a constantly running tap and a waste system that takes your water away. If I'm in the country or in some out-of-the-way spot, I will boil a kettle, use a bowl and have a wash and shave outside. Water was thrown discreetly away. We never see the need to waste gas by turning the hot water on, all this and other saving methods just come naturally to us, mind, that's because we spend a lot of time travelling, over the years you learn to economise and compromise. Clearly, a different attitude would and could be adopted by someone who only uses their motorhome for two or three weeks a year plus the odd weekend, but then if they are spending many thousands of pounds on a motorhome, then they might have a different mindset, we are all different, and we all have a different way of looking at things.

A much bigger problem we find is the emptying of the toilet cassette waste. First, if we're taking the kids or grandkids away for a break, we choose places where we know there are public toilets, Llandudno or Barmouth being just two examples. But that's only for two or three-day breaks. For longer breaks, we go to a campsite. Alternatively, some caravan and camping sites will allow you on, specifically to dump your waste, for a small fee, of course. Another logical step that many people take is to just book into a site every three or four days or when considered adequate. This enables you to connect to the electricity, shower, empty waste, fill up with water, charge batteries and use all facilities before heading off on the next part of your journey.

MOTORHOME
CARAVAN OR STATIC

The best and wisest move we ever made was buying our motorhome. It could have turned out to have been a big mistake. We had never had the experience of one before. Our nearest experience was our one-tonne builder's van we used to clean out before heading off on our travels. Once the idea occurred to us and we started looking at various models, we enjoyed the idea. Once we saw the ones with the garages on the back, we were hooked.

For years we had toyed with the idea of buying and owning a static. Our own little furnished holiday home by the sea or in the country. A dream come true if you live in a private or council house. The problem is, it's not all it's cracked up to be. First, it's not even your van. Oh, it's your van, alright, or you think it is, until you come to sell it, then a whole host of rules and regulations come into play. First, you see the van. Maybe it's advertised or being sold by a friend of a friend. A favourite destination for us Brummies is Stourport or Bewdley. Right on the river with fishing or entertainment within a short walk. One or two friends have bought static vans on these sites, and I know they have and still enjoy many happy and enjoyable little breaks. One pal living in a council house in the inner city bought a lovely little static in Stourport for five grand. I know in his case, he was thrilled. An hour's drive from his home, he could relax in the local clubhouse and town before going back to his own little home by the river. In his case, it worked out well. If he ever sold it, I know he would accept the loss that selling it would entail.

First, some, if not most or all, site owners insist on being given the first option or offer to buy it. I have known this offer to be less than half of what was paid for the van or was worth. If they find a private buyer, they are whacked that hard. They may as well have sold it to the site owners. Many a seller leaves the site with a little bitterness in their mouths. Then there is how many times you're going to use the static van, your second home. Some sites only charge some £3,000 per year, i.e. some £60 per week, not a lot if you say it quickly and you're using it some fifty-two weeks of the year. If you're only using it for one or two months of the year, it becomes almost as expensive as a 4-star hotel in London. Then there are the running expenses, the gas, electric hook-up, etc. These can add an extra £30 a week to the costings. Once in Spain on a campsite, after we had bought our own motorhome, I got chatting with a few of the static owners who were not happy bunnies at all. They had brought the mobile homes before Brexit, and when the euro was at a high, we were getting 1.60 to the pound, with the euro having the same buying power as the pound. Some of these folks had bought their static vans for some sixty grand, having sold their homes for one hundred grand, leaving them with forty grand in their pocket and a pension of £300 per week. All very nice if things remained as they were, but they didn't.

Within a few years, the static vans had more than halved in value. The euro had dropped to near enough an equal par, one pound one euro, yet the Spanish prices crept up. Whilst the ground rent was only £3,000 per year, the little extras like gas, electric, etc. added an extra £40 per week. The site owner, known throughout the camp as Mr Ten Per Cent because of his penchant for putting that amount on everything and every bit of work carried out on the site. Car breakdown? He wanted ten per cent of the mechanic who came onto the site to carry out repairs. Yes, the man was a businessman, alright.

If you didn't maintain and keep the static van up to standard, you were made quite clear of the consequences. Owners diligently kept their vans well-maintained. If your partner died, and it happened a few times, the pensions halved. Left with £50 a week after paying their site fees, the belts had to be well tightened. We spoke to the pensioner who had to sell up for what she could get before returning home to her children. The couple whose partners had died and felt the only option was to move in with each other, even though they didn't like each other, shudder, shudder.

My initial feeling of stopping on the site was how fantastic it all looked. Thankfully, I saw the other side. My ex-brother-in-law had a static caravan on a small site near Weston-Super-Mare. Ordered to remove it because of its age and condition, and he and his wife had to literally beg the owner to allow them to keep it, which he reluctantly did on the promise that they maintained it more diligently. Terrified, they agreed and were down there at every opportunity. Having a couple of friends who lived on a site opposite, they were horrified to hear of their circumstances. The husband died; the wife could not visit their static for several months. When she did, she found her caravan gone and her belongings dumped to the side of the pitch in black bin bags. Distraught, the owner told her he had put a letter through her caravan door, all legal, and there was nothing she could do about it. No, buying a static was not for us.

We had looked at caravans a few years before we bought our motorhome, even buying a second-hand one to try it out. First, I discovered the idea of towing a caravan behind me was not for me. Then we quickly realised you couldn't just tootle off. We had to book in advance to know we had got a site to go to. A three-hour drive to, say, Barmouth that normally took three hours doubled when towing a caravan. The idea of visiting southern Spain was a definite no-go. The only definite positive was the fact that once we were in our own little home on our own little pitch, we were free to use it as a base to tour the local area. No, owning a caravan was not for us either. We were in limbo till we saw and found the motorhome. Complete freedom to go where we wanted and when we wanted, on-site or wild camping wherever we wanted. Bliss!

TINTAGEL AND BODMIN MOOR

Tintagel to the northwest was half on the mainland and half on the jagged headland. Tintagel Castle is one of the most historic sites in Britain, home to the famous legend of King Arthur and the Knights of the Round Table. History and legend go hand in hand here. An important stronghold from the 5th and 7th centuries and the residence of many Cornwall rulers. Many fragments of luxury pottery were found here imported from the Mediterranean. Whether King Arthur was a true Cornish king or a legend dreamt up and written about by the 12th-century writer Geoffrey of Monmouth in his history of the kings of Britain is debatable, but it doesn't matter. We who want to believe, believe. I believe Sean Connery was the real king of Camelot. I just feel it was a terrible act of betrayal that Lancelot did the dirty on him by having an affair behind his back. At any rate, the castle now in ruins was built by Richard the Earl of Cornwall in the 1230s, or thereabouts.

To get to the castle originally would have been a mission in itself, built as it was on the jagged headland, deliberately so. But the council, in their wisdom, built a 225ft steel bridge in 2019. The walk across is awe-inspiring. Food and drink are available from the beach café, plus there is a picnic area with fantastic views overlooking the coast where you can enjoy your own food and drinks. Although run by English Heritage, the castle and land are owned by King Charles, well, probably by Prince William now. They do like to keep it in the family, those royals.

The village itself, or Trevena to give it its Cornish name, is well worth a visit, but its fame comes from association and closeness to the castle just a few hundred yards away. There are a couple of pottery shops and galleries in the village and gift shops and cafes. At the lower end of the village is a steep track that leads down through the Vale of Avalon and onto the very roots of the castle Merlin's Cave, also used by the inevitable smugglers. From here, you get another magnificent view of the coast. The old medieval building in the heart of the village now holds the post office and is well worth a little nose, as are the well-maintained gardens.

Well worth a visit is King Arthur's great halls, the Halls of Chivalry. Amazingly, these halls were built in homage to King Arthur at great expense by a millionaire whose grandfather owned the Monk and Glass Custard Factory in partnership with the grandfather of Bob Monkhouse. With laser lights and an imposing granite throne, it's also licenced as a wedding venue.

The thing I find fascinating about Cornwall and even Devon is the number of fruitcakes, ding-bats and nut jobs that abound. Maybe it's the mysticism, the legends, the myths and the stories that abound in every village, cove and bay. There is the Living Mermaid, the Lady of Tintagel, and the lizard who believes she is a mermaid. Morris dancers abound in almost every village. This practice dates back to medieval times and involved a group of men in strange garb, straw hats and carrying sticks dancing in a circle. Then you have the worshipper of the stones. Pagan followers who meet up and gather to worship at the stones like Stonehenge dotted around the country, many of them around Cornwall, told you there were a lot of funny currents around there.

Padstow is a beautiful fishing port on the north coast of Cornwall, just a few miles from Tintagel and on the west bank of the River Camel, just a few miles from Bodmin and ten miles from Newquay. Padstow is a working harbour and fishing port with some great beaches and a kind attitude to campers as long as a bit of discretion is used. Whilst the fishing has declined over the years, the town has boomed since Rick Stein, the chef, returned to the town and put it on the map. Once just another little fishing and seaport amongst hundreds of other little fishing and seaports, when Rick set up shop, he brought it to prominence with his television programmes and fresh seafood restaurant. Initially, it's easy to see that Rick, being a Padstow boy, was the town's saviour and as popular as he could be. A television celebrity, a star, he was a shining light in the town, but as his popularity grew, so did his ambition to buy up more properties and more businesses. As his fame grew, so did the price of properties in the town. Initially pleased with their growing investments, the local townspeople were full of praise for Rick, but soon the prices became more than the locals could afford. I sometimes have the impression that Rick is no longer the most popular guy in Padstow.

Bodmin Moor itself is a fascinating and atmospheric place with stories that just seep through its history. Having camped over and on it many times, you almost expect the Hound of the Baskervilles to jump out at any moment. Some nearly 200 square miles in size, it includes Brown Willy, the highest point in Cornwall. Many of Cornwall's rivers are sourced from here. Bodmin contains countless ancient monuments such as the hurlers, the tripper stones and countless other cairns and settlements. It is easy to stand looking at them and transport yourself back to those premedieval times and imagine those local villagers coming out to worship and dancing around them. To the southeast lies the Cornish mining world heritage site, which is well worth a visit.

Bodmin Moor is the go-to place for walks, hiking and trails, from pleasant short woodland walks to strenuous hikes.

Deserted as it may seem, there are thousands of people who live on Bodmin moor itself with many villages and hamlets, all living happily with the infamous Beast of Bodmin living within its midst. The biggest jewel on Bodmin moor is the famous Jamaica Inn, made even more famous by Alfred Hitchcock in the film made famous by Daphne du Maurier's Tale of Murder and Smuggling. Jamaica Inn is well worth a visit with its character, atmosphere and artefacts littered around the place. Visiting or stopping on a foggy night like Daphne du Maurier did is a visit that will stay in your memory forever.

With our hotel in north Devon, it was just a short drive for us to reach the Bodmin moor for camping breaks. Bodmin is just made for camping, whether in a tent or the motorhome. Our first breaks over the moor used to be in a tent where I could pretend to be Davey Crockett, King of the Wild Frontier. Unfortunately, I never allowed for the fact that I had two young girls with us who just couldn't get their heads around taking a shovel behind the nearest mound or bush, digging a hole and doing their business, well I didn't know, did I. After two enjoyable nights where I could fulfil my fantasies of sitting around the campfire singing Home on the Range, alone, we found the nearest campsite for the next couple of nights. This brought us up to Camelford, some 14 miles from Jamaica Inn and a short distance inland from Tintagel. This made my wife, Bet and kids very happy with the toilet and shower facilities on site. It helped that it had a friendly bar as well. Behind the campsite itself, the owner, together with his partner, ran an animal sanctuary/zoo that contained all kinds of animals in their own enclosures. Deer, varieties of sheep and goats, ostriches, buffalos and ponies, plus many more. The kids fell in love with the place, and so did we. Becoming friendly with the owner.

We had visited zoos before, of course. One of our favourites and most natural environments was Twycross Zoo in the midlands, but springing up on us as it did, this struck us as more informal, even more natural. The kids naturally fell in love with it. The surroundings of Bodmin Moor seemed to influence all of us. This didn't escape the attention of the owners, who were equally impressed with our love for the place. Somehow we left the site on the friendliest of terms and the assurance that if the place ever came onto the market, we could be very well interested in it. Some months later, and just before we had put our hotel up for sale, I answered the phone to the owner, who asked if we might still be interested in the venture. Upon my affirmative response, he then mentioned a price, but just for the campsite alone, not the rest of the land or the animal farm. This put us in a bit of a quandary. The campsite and bar would be a stand-alone venue reliant on the animal farm bringing in customers. What would be the percentage of customers visiting the farm simply for a few hours or the day against someone looking to stop for a night or two, maybe longer, using the site as a base to explore Bodmin and the nearby amenities?

Any accounts would just be guesswork, as they could be worked around in any way the sellers wanted. We knew that the owners and sellers were genuine, but they were asking for a great deal of money indeed. Far more than we would have expected just for what was a small isolated campsite with a bar on Bodmin moor. What if they closed the farm down five minutes after we had bought the place? The other factor that worried us was the schooling for the kids. Bodmin was 14 miles away. Where were the nearest schools? Once the initial excitement was over, how would they feel about it then? With some reluctance, we decided it wouldn't be a good idea to go any further with the idea. To the day I die, I will always wonder if we made the right decision. But that is the gamble in life that many of us can be faced with when it comes to bringing children up. We have heard of or spoken to people who have picked their kids up and taken them around the world, some on yachts, some in motorhomes. Who is to judge who is doing the best for their children? We had come to a crossroads a few times in our lives, giving us pause for thought.

Some 17 miles north of Camelford lay Widemouth Bay and then Bude, still in Cornwall but just short of north Devon. On the Atlantic Coast, Bude is long and flat, with nearly a mile of soft-level sand. It also has a man-made, free-to-enter tidal swimming pool or lido in the rocks at Summerleaze Beach. Bude has something for everyone with great fish-n-chips, fudge, cream scones and the ever-present Cornish pasty. But Bude is perhaps more known for its surfing than anything else, attracting young folks from around the world looking to strut their stuff on their surfboards all year round. We found quite a few places along the main seafront road and off the A39, with a relaxed attitude by the locals. This was probably in part due to all the young dudes coming in their dozens with their surfboards and camper vans, parking up anywhere. Surrounded by miles of countryside, Bude and its surrounding area certainly have something for all age groups.

For want of something to do one New Year's Eve, we had looked around to see which seaside town held the best seaside celebrations. We had tired a little of the same old same old, visiting friends or family to celebrate. This usually comprised meeting up at one's house, bringing a bottle, and saying the usual hellos, happy new year etc. etc., most times. They are great. The food is laid out, the drinks flow, and then, the anti-climax. Many times, as hosts, we might try to vary it by inviting occasional friends, hoping it might lift others up. It doesn't work. It doesn't help that almost every year, the country seems to be in some kind of recession that affects one or more. I tell you, the Queen doesn't know what an *annus horribilis* is. Every year is an *annus horribilis* for some, well, except for the Scots. Of course, to hear people talk, the Scots have a fantastic New Year's Eve. I have been to that many New Year's Eve parties that have died a death five minutes after midnight. Some before that, I have lost count.

The south coast seaside resorts were some of the few places we hadn't visited, Mevagissey Fowey, along with Hastings and Folkestone. All great and interesting places to holiday and/or visit. Two places that came up as good venues for New Year's Eve were Looe and Weymouth. Looe put on a very nice New Year's Eve display. Even better, we were able to enjoy the full benefit of it by parking overnight on the harbour front right by the war memorial. The fireworks displays were very impressive as the whole town came out to take part and enjoy the atmosphere. Looe, some 45 minutes from Plymouth, is divided in two by the River Looe and connected by a beautiful stone bridge that links East and West. Approached from high cliffs, we dropped into the beautiful resort and seafront, a very good sized, soft sandy beach leading onto the azure blue sea. Without a doubt, Looe is stunning, with hotels and houses rising high above. It has a delightful array of gift shops, restaurants, fresh seafood stalls and traditional fish-n-chips and pasties.

Some of the best pasties we had were at the Looe bakery on Fore Street, right alongside the River Looe that opened out onto the sea. What helped, of course, was nibbling on them while sitting on a bench alongside the river, people-watching, and just soaking up the ambience of the place. Just a few yards further along was the bridge café where we could enjoy a nice pot of tea or coffee to wash the pasty down whilst doing a bit more people-watching. Summer or winter, the experience was something to enjoy with the sun beating down, unbeatable.

We found Looe a never-ending maze of little narrow side streets and back allies, a bit of a surprise, really, as from one perspective, it doesn't look that big. Facing off and well worth a visit is George Island, famed for its use by smugglers in days of old. It can be reached by foot at low tide. Like most Cornish resorts, driving around Looe, especially in the harbour's vicinity and old boathouse, is a bit of a no-no at the height of summer. I'd best forget it. It's a case of getting in early, finding a spot to park up, then forgetting it and not moving until late in the day. The views from the harbour out to sea from along the stone pier and back towards the land with the high cliffs, houses, and hotels are stunning, with Looe retaining all the charm of the traditional Victorian seaside resort.

Some nine or ten miles from Looe is Portwrinkle, a small fishing/coastal village. There is no access at the western end of Whitesand Bay. The harbour itself is popular with divers and kayakers, which makes motorboats and jet skis a no. No access to the harbour by car, certainly not by our motorhome so it's a case of parking up in the village car park which has toilets. If you want peace and tranquillity, a nice shingle beach with the sound of the surf lapping at your feet, then Portwrinkle is as good a place as you can get. The east beach is great for surfing by experienced surfers only, but Portwrinkle is famous for its pilchards and pilchards cellars. Incorporated into the 17th-century walls of the pilchard cellars, now transformed into housing. Although the village has a harbour and two beaches, it has no shops. Apart from the beach car park, it's quiet.

Seaton, just a few miles further along, is different and busier. Yet another small village a few miles from Looe at the mouth of the River Seaton. Seaton Beach is mostly shingle. We visited the Seaton Valley Countryside Park, one of the first in the country to receive a green flag. Its car park can get full in the summer, but even in the low season, we found it difficult to find somewhere to park in our motorhome.

DARTMOOR NATIONAL PARK

For a complete change of direction, but arriving from the north on a specific visit, we travelled to Dartmoor National Park. To me, when Dartmoor is mentioned, all I can think of is Sherlock Holmes and the Hound of the Baskervilles and Dartmoor Prison. Well, it doesn't take a lot of brains, does it? Put the two together, and Dartmoor doesn't sound like a place to visit. Cold, isolated, prone to mist enveloping vast swathes of the place, prisoners on the loose. Wrong.

Dartmoor is a fantastic place to visit, see, tour and hike. Best of all, us campers and motorhome owners are free to wild camp almost anywhere along and on its moors, historically laid down in ancient law. Course, I'd advise locking up whilst you're in the prison's vicinity. The things to see and do are many, with just a short list here.

PENNYWELL FARM. It is an award-winning farm packed full of animal attractions, activities, shows and displays. Considered the biggest activity farm in the southwest, it's well worth a visit. It's easy to see why it won the top visitor attraction in the southwest two years on the trot. Join in the activities like goat milking, ferret racing and deer feeding, egg collecting and lots more. This is home to the world-famous Pennywell miniature pigs. For an enormous treat, don't miss the famous Pennywell Pig Race for plenty of snorting, snotting and squealing. Allow at least three hours to see and experience everything.

BUCKFAST BUTTERFLY FARM AND OTTER SANCTUARY. This is a great way to spend the best part of the day. The first things you see are the butterflies, free-flying and totally beautiful. The otters are a treat to watch and so funny, a bonus is you can adopt an otter, and there are two feeding times. Outside the sanctuary are a play area for the children and a café up by the train station, which sells hot food, teas and coffees. From here, you can take the steam train to Totness and back. Both together, a wonderful and full day out.

LYDFORD GORGE. Not for the infirm or faint-hearted, this is a terrific walk and experience. One of the best places to lose yourself for a few hours. The gorge, the myriad sounds of running water, the various animals and plants, from the treetops down to the river. A great day out, but my advice is to take it steady. By the time we got back, we were shattered.

BUCKFAST ABBEY. If you like medieval architecture, stained glass windows and a bit of history, you will get your fill here. The interior is awe-inspiring, beautiful gardens to lose yourself. They rebuilt the abbey in the mid-20th century. Very peaceful and well worth visiting, even just to hear the monks singing, and it's all free.

CANONTEIGN FALLS. This is another fantastic place to visit. Even just to sit and immerse yourself in the mystical silence and tranquillity of the Victorian Fern Gardens while listening to the top of the falls close by. It's a steep climb in places, again not for the infirm, but the views from the top are stunning and well worth the climb. The descent back is easy enough, with a pleasant little café at the bottom for refreshments. If you're still breathing, you will need them.

MINATURE PONY CENTRE. For the kids, this is a great place to visit. We had a few days with our grandkids when we gave this a visit. No child dislikes ponies, and few adults either, allow for plenty of *oohs* and *ahhs*. With lots of ponies to love and cuddle, plenty of enjoyable walks, and a play area too. The staff were friendly and enthusiastic, the pony rides were good, and the prices were reasonable.

RIVER DART COUNTRY PARK. To be frank, the River Dart Country Park reminded me of the Cannock Chase Park in Staffordshire, only bigger. Sweeping woodlands, high rope climbing courses, bike trails, and BMX tracks. There is a campsite where you can spend a few nights or as long as you want to fill your boots with all the adrenaline-filled exercises you could want. The original main house now doubles as a hotel, so if you want a break from the camper or the tent, you can book in there for a night or two. It might be well deserved after a couple of days of busting your guts on what it has to offer.

BURRATOR RESERVOIR. A place of natural beauty, the reservoir has a nice circular walk that will get your adrenalin and your appetite built up.

BUCKLAND ABBEY. This is a fascinating and informative historic site to visit. Beautiful gardens, a tithe barn well worth visiting and plenty of history, and a nice little café which allows you to chill, relax and soak up the atmosphere. A bonus is all the history and information about the life and times of Sir Francis Drake. Run by the national trust, together with its volunteers, who were very helpful. Sometimes, you have to say, 'Thank you, Lord', for the national trust.

TAVISTOCK PANNIER MARKET. In the very heart of Tavistock is the ancient and medieval Pannier Market, going back over 900 years. The market is open all year round, with interchangeable traders operating five days a week throughout the year, a must-see tourist attraction.

DARTMOOR PRISON AND MUSEUM. Situated opposite the prison is the museum which gives a fascinating insight into prison life yesteryear and today. My knowledge of it was like most people, from what I had read in the newspapers. Prisoners were escaping or working in work parties over the moors. How the locals felt about that, god knows. The moors were so barren, isolated and unwelcoming few prisoners could escape, which would, I bet, be very comforting. The history of the prison is all visible from the work on show by the prisoners, like prison bags? So harsh you have to wonder how anyone could leave and not be expected to go back. What encouragement not to lead a respectful life. That's if you got out alive, of course. The mind boggles at the thought of the harsh treatment meted out to prisoners daily. How many bodies are buried on those moors, *ay*? As well as the museum showing the history of the prison, it also sells items and goods made by the prisoners, with all proceeds going back into the prison service itself. We gave that a miss. The nearby Highwayman Inn says it all about Dartmoor.

Covering some 116,000 acres of unenclosed common land and open country, the special quality here is the freedom to roam and stop where you want, within reason and away from the roads. On the open moor, you are free to choose where to walk without the need to stick to footpaths. Bliss! Complete freedom. The friendly staff at Buckland Abbey told us that there were toilets spread out over the moors, but we found one. Mind, we weren't really looking. Thankfully, we were completely self-contained with our own toilet, washing up facilities, fridge and cooker, so we were fine over the moors for days at a time. Certainly, Dartmoor is a place we would visit again and again.

From Seaton to Dover, there are still many places to visit, stay and experience. Just along the coast from Seaton is Lyme Regis, leading on some 30 miles to Weymouth. Lyme Regis is yet another active fishing harbour and holiday resort, but more than that, Lyme Regis sits on the Jurassic coast. This 95-mile stretch of coast is a world heritage site, so it's a hotspot for fossil hunting.

The town beach is a sand and shingle beach along the curving bay, ideal for swimming. It's probably the busiest beach on hot, sunny days. Monmouth Beach to the west is another shingle beach and home to the famous ammonite pavement containing ammonite fossils, the cliff beach, another shingle beach with patches of sand (the most popular) which sits on the mouth of the River Lym. Low tide exposes plenty of rock pools, which are great for kids. East Cliff Beach is fossil-rich and runs east towards Charmouth. The cliffs above can be dangerous and liable to collapse at any time, but on a positive note, they also provide the fossils found regularly on the beach. Lyme Regis is a hotspot for fossil hunting.

Lyme was the home of famed palaeontologist and fossil collector Mary Anning. No, me neither. The museum is a great place and well worth a visit for its brilliant fossil collections and the life story of Mary Anning. The main street, or Cobb, skirts around the lovely little bay, a curving breakwater built to protect the harbour. The thick stone wall provides stunning views of the pretty bay and harbour, with plenty of beach huts. The wall has been featured in many films and TV adaptions, including The French Lieutenant's Woman. The Cobb is also home to the marine aquarium.

With plenty of shops, boutiques and art galleries, there is plenty to see, do and spend your money on. Nestled in the town's artisan quarter lies the town's flower mill. Dating from at least the 1300s, the medieval watermill is still running and creating stone ground flour. Guided tours are offered daily in exchange for a small donation to the mill's charitable trust. The mill also acts as a home for several businesses, i.e. art galleries, studios and a café.

Great hiking can be had along the Jurassic coast, like the three-mile hike along the inland cliff path coming back along the beach. The Hix Oyster and Fish House opened and run by local chef Mark Hix, is all about locally sourced fish and seafood. My cod was very nice, but I thought a tad expensive for the size served. The Alexandra Hotel is a nice place to spend the afternoon with a pot of tea and fantastic views of the bay. Built for the Dowager Countess Poulett in 1735, the building became a hotel in 1901. A great place to chill and relax, and not as expensive as the Hix.

Known as the pearl of Dorset (these resorts do like bigging themselves up a bit), it has plenty to offer for everyone, but there is also plenty to do around and outside the town. The Undercliffs is a 304-hectare national nature reserve between Lyme Regis and Axemouth. The only access route is along the southwest coastal path. Nearby is the Axe Valley Wildlife Park, a small friendly zoo in Axminster, great for the kids and close to Lyme for a day out.

Weymouth, further along from Lyme Regis and between Exeter and Bournemouth on the peninsular, is another very nice and interesting resort. Like Lyme Regis, dotted with colourful beach huts and backed by stunning Georgian houses (Why do these Southerners love their beach huts so much?). Some of them can cost as much, if not more, than a house. You can't live in them. They are just garden sheds, yet they love them. Do they sit in them out of the sun or rain? Keep all three deckchairs tables and cutlery in them? Must do. Weymouth is in Dorset, on the Devon border, and is often described as the Naples of England. Told you these resorts love their little nicknames, the Pearl of the South, the English Riviera. Weymouth is the Italian Naples of England. Originally a fishing village, it became a tourist destination in the 17th century when King George visited the resort and bought Gloucester Lodge, built by his brother, the Duke of Gloucester (they keep it in the family, those royals).

Many of the buildings date from that time and even have a very nice Georgian esplanade overlooking Weymouth Bay. With a long sandy beach, safe bathing and stunning scenery, it's ideally situated to explore the surrounding countryside.

Vying with other resorts, Weymouth has plenty for everyone. The donkeys on the beach are a favourite attraction, but there are lots more; the beach kite festival, motorcycle and vintage vehicle rallies. There is the iron man triathlon sailing championships, handball and volleyball events, and then there is the main event of the year, carnival day in August. But to us, the big one was the New Year's Eve Party.

A bit of a distance for us for one night, we made it a three-day event over the new year, first calling into Looe, watching the buildup to the new year whilst enjoying an evening meal down by the harbour. Driving into Weymouth, our problem was finding somewhere to park. Our motorhome, whilst not big, big, isn't small either.

The whole of the seafront road was barricaded off, but a friendly cop guided us onto the double yellow lines at the far end, telling us to enjoy the night and not to worry. The town was out in force and building up. All the pubs were bursting at the seams, as were the burger bars and kiosks. Halfway along was a live band set up alongside the beach and pavement, everyone in good spirits. The atmosphere was brilliant. Locking our motorhome up, we set off enjoying the night, mingling with the locals and drinking in the bars. The live band was fantastic, and the fireworks display at midnight was one of the best we had seen, but we watched it from our motorhome whilst enjoying a nice bottle of wine. Drunk in charge?? In all the years I have been driving around Europe or England, I have never had a problem with having a drink in our motorhome. In Weymouth, the police themselves had pointed me to the double yellow lines, so I knew we would not be bothered for the night.

Of course, common sense must prevail. I would not be so stupid as to expect to pull onto double yellow lines at any other time, even more so at the height of the season. Neither would I expect to park in a busy area, either in England or abroad. In France, there are Aires (free spaces) every few miles, specifically set out for camper vans. It is only when I know we are in a secure safe place I will settle down to have a drink. Mind, in the early days of buying our motorhome, I made that mistake in a wooded off-road area outside Weston-Super-Mare before being told to move on. Unbeknown to me, it was private land.

The fort overlooking Weymouth Harbour is a key landmark, built in 1860 to ward off French invasions. It has an interesting museum. The harbour itself is beautiful with coloured houses, fishing boats and the inevitable but welcome chip shops. Dating from the 16th century, the focus here is just to sit and enjoy.

Chesil Beach stands in contrast to Weymouth Beach, and a special experience is watching the sunrise or sunset. Sand World is another seasonal experience with artists working on new pieces underneath a marquee building. Amazing works of art out of the sand.

On Preston Beach Road lies the sea life adventure park with a whole range of sea dwellers, including otters, penguins and octopuses. St Albans Street is a fascinating shopping centre full of Georgian shops and houses.

Durdle Door is a scene of outstanding natural beauty sitting next to the shingle beach, a UNESCO World Heritage Site. It's just as famous for its many deaths of young lads jumping off the rocks by misjudging the tidal waters. If they don't die, they can end up paralyzed for life.

THE ISLE OF WIGHT
AND BOGNOR REGIS

The Isle of Wight has always intrigued me. What is it? A small island. What is its purpose? It's an island some half a mile from the mainland that should take 15 minutes to get to and, for some reason, takes an hour. When we were in the hotel business, I noticed their prices were very cheap, with all kinds of deals going on with free ferry tickets etc., but then every hotel was struggling.

There was nothing to appeal to me about the island to want to make an effort until my good friend, Micky Kirby, asked me to visit. Rather than use the motorhome, we drove over in the car. I'm glad we did. Why doesn't someone build a bridge? Failing that, why not a pathway with two brick walls on either side to keep the sea out? Surely, at its deepest point, it can't be that deep. At some stage, it would obviously have been attached to the mainland.

First, we had to wait for the ferry, then drive on, and then wait. When the ferry set off, I assumed it would just paddle across in a straight line, which was directly in front of us, but no, it set off slowly in a major curve. What's all that about then? Getting off was just as bad, with a sharp bend and curve before finally getting away.

My pal lived in Shanklin, on a campsite, of all things. He had bought a nice little chalet in order to get away from it all, from

Birmingham, from the city, from England. Walking around the seafront at Shanklin did not leave me overwhelmed. The best thing to come out of it was a couple of crabs that Micky had treated us to, which turned out to be the best freshest crab we had ever eaten in our lives. The holiday chalet site comprised hundreds of chalets and a bar entertainment complex. Any other leisure facilities had now long gone, a sign of how the leisure industry had deteriorated over the years. The chalets are sold off to individuals as investments or for letting.

The island is noted for its nice beaches, so we set off to discover the island. Ventnor was pretty, and Ventnor Beach, with its beach huts dotted around, was quite attractive. Spanning 13.5 miles north to south and 22.5 miles east to west, the island didn't take long to get around.

There are 57 miles of coast, twenty beaches, woodland and a nature reserve. 50 attractions and places to visit. With its mild climate, it's been a popular holiday destination since Victorian times, around the same time as the mainland. Then, it holds some of the UK's leading events like the Isle of Wight Festival, the world's largest rock festival, not forgetting the world-famous Cowes Week sailing regatta. Just a couple of miles from Cowes is the HMP, Parkhurst Prison. I doubt those inmates feel they are on holiday.

Once an independent country in the 15th century, it was England's smallest county when the tide was in. Sandown was built and occupied by the Romans and is one of the finest Roman sites in the UK. After the Romans came the Jutes, then the Anglo-Saxons, and then the Danes, who were then conquered by the Normans. They established and built Carisbrooke Castle, where King Charles I was held before having his head chopped off in 1649.

The island was part of Hampshire until 1890, before it became a county in its own right. Queen Victoria was very fond of the island and lived in Osbourne House. Now open to the public. Her patronage made the island popular as a holiday resort. Ventnor, Sandown and Ryde sprang up to cater for a large number of visitors.

The needles are a sight worth seeing, with three chalk stacks rising from the sea. Alum Bay is famous for its sand cliffs, and so is the Calbourne Water Mill and museum. The Shipwreck Museum we found was well worth viewing. It also has Amazon World, the Wildheart Animal Sanctuary, Isle of Wight Monkey Haven and Butterfly World. Great, if you like butterflies. The Godshill Model Village was very enjoyable, rounded off by a trip on the Havenstreet Steam Railway.

There is plenty to see and do on the Isle of Wight for a week or a fortnight. My friend loves it that much. He went to live there, mind his family had already been there for a few years. His ex-wife is running a pub there, so it obviously appeals to some people. Personally, I didn't feel it was worth all the hassle of getting the ferry over onto it. The motorhome owner might feel different, as I realised there were plenty of places to camp overnight as well as there being campsites.

Bognor Regis, 55 miles from London and 24 miles from Brighton, sits in West Sussex and is classed as a town, and it's a big town that I feel felt more like a city that has seen better days. With its 2.7-mile-long promenade and its long sandy beach, it's close to the South Downs National Park castles like Arundel Castle and country houses. The beaches are great places to spend a day, with East Beach, Felpham Beach, Aldwick, and Pagham. It also has plenty of open spaces and parks. Hotham Park holds plenty of events, including proms, the country fair music festivals and even its own miniature railway station and a boating lake. Turquoise, the sea, is great for swimming. The beaches are shingle and uncomfortable. The long promenade seems to go on for miles, far more than its actual distance, passing hotels, shops and seafront amusements. The traffic noise is endless. From the pier built in the mid-1830s, the views across the beach and towards the town are, well, maybe not exciting. Flat and level, there are some great walks for those looking to keep fit, like me. Uphill walking is not my favourite hobby. I found the town centre boring. You could be in any city in the world. The only sign you were by the sea was the seagulls.

Maybe it's an age thing with me. When I was in my late teens and early twenties, I spent twelve months in Chiswick, London, and didn't find it appealing at all. People walk around like strangers rushing to get from one place to the next. Growing up in Birmingham, my dad was a barrow boy in the old Bullring. It was a time and a place where everyone knew each other; we knew our neighbours. Today it's a lot different. Whilst still friendly, it's losing its intimacy. At any rate, having known that friendliness and intimacy and meeting the coldness and bustle of London, I'm naturally averse to anything coming close to it.

Driving through Spain or France, cities like Paris, Madrid or Barcelona are just not on my radar. Paris, Versailles, amazing and beautiful, and my wife and I enjoyed them twice on four-day mini breaks by coach, but sitting behind the driver was awful; the roads were horrendous. Every other car had a dent. Apparently, the French consider it par for the course and don't even report it. So no, when I'm driving anywhere, I just put into my sat-nav, avoid.

Bognor is one of those places. When I go to a seaside resort, I like to relax, chill, and walk along without a care in the world, enjoying the ambience and atmosphere. My only enjoyable experience of Bognor was working at Butlins more years ago than I care to remember.

Being young and fancy-free with no responsibilities, I enjoyed a couple of years around the country, finding my feet and my niche. One such year, me and a pal headed to give Butlins a look over. Sited just outside the town of Bognor, Butlins was a big place surrounded by ten-foot chain link fencing. Most people assume the fencing is to keep interlopers out. No, no, no, we who worked there quickly found out that it was to keep the holidaymakers in, to stop them from escaping. Being young and almost skint, we had arrived late and had nowhere to stay overnight before applying inside for a job. Mooching around, we found a break in the chain link and let ourselves in before making our way to the bar.

It didn't take us long to get chatting with some scot lads in the Pig and Whistle bar. These were Gorbals boys from Glasgow, friendly, effusive, and helpful. When I mentioned I had nowhere to stay for the night, they turned and told me not to worry; I think it helped that they'd had a few bevvies. At closing time, they told us to follow them, and they led us to their accommodation, which was hidden away above the shops in the centre of the camp. Walking along the corridors and past cheap little windowless rooms, they stopped at one, gave it a sharp kick, and the door burst open. Pointing to the beds, we were told to "get in their boys and have a good night's sleep" in that gruff but friendly Gorbals chime. "See ya tomorrow."

Getting up the next day, we made our way to the main reception offices. Without further ado, the guy in charge gave us a quick look up and down, mentioned security, and gave us the traditional blue fit-all-size uniform. We were now camp security, private police officers. Well, I never gave it a thought. Setting off and putting the uniform on in our allocated chalet, near to the offices and not as I might have expected in the grotty rooms above the shops, we set off for work.

Security was a great little job, as I had found out doing security at Butlins Skegness. It was a girl magnet. It wasn't work, really. Walking around all day, looking professional, the odds of having any trouble were negligible. Large groups of single holidaymakers were banned, and the last thing most families wanted was trouble. They were spending money on having a good time. With food included, I had cracked it. Until I bumped into the jocks.

Seeing them over at the bar in the Pig and Whistle, I sauntered across with a big smile on my mush. It soon disappeared. After looking at me with a blank stare, they pulled a face, grunted and abruptly turned their backs on me. I was now the enemy and thick as two planks, I never even realised. With their Gorbals razor cut scars, I decided it was best to do an about-turn and walk away. We never spoke again, but tensions rose on more than one occasion as their machismo was put to the test.

In my leisure time, I thought it prudent to spend my time away from the camp and away from the Gorbals boys drinking in the local pubs around the town, that is, of course, when I wasn't entertaining the girls who were attracted to the little blue uniform. Guys, guys, it's just a job. I'm not a real cop. I wouldn't want to be a real cop. After a couple of months of still being uncomfortable around the jocks and not particularly enjoying the town of Bognor Regis, I moved on to other chimes.

The next destination from Bognor was Margate, where I had been offered a job running a stall in the local dreamland entertainment complex. After getting some cheap digs in a boarding house on one of the side streets, I turned up to start work on the stall. Running, it was a slick old boy who had the gift of the gab and the ability to draw the punters in. At his side was a very attractive-looking girl with black wavy hair and blue eyes. Giving her a quick once over, I thought my luck might be in for later. Behind these two was a large circular disc with records placed in a circle around the disc. The idea was to draw the punters in and invite them to toss a dice and guess which record would be played once the disc stopped; the odds were about 200 to 1.

The girl was part of the draw, the eye candy. She was, indeed. I was to be trained up by the old boy and act as backup, drawing the punters in. "Come on, folks, who's going to be brave enough to try his luck on the big wheel?" "Pick a record and win a prize from anywhere on the stall." The prizes were good, and the old guy had the gift of the gab; he was going to be a hard act to follow. By the end of the first month, I got the hang of it.

What a little money maker that stall was, the whole of Dreamland was amazing. It was massive with every fun ride or game you could think of designed to suck every shilling out of your pockets, slides, big wheels, bumper cars and stalls, the idea being you went in with your pockets full and left with them empty. My job was to help empty them.

The job was great, the pay decent, and just like my job on security at Butlins Bognor, I quickly found it a little babe magnet. It amazed me how many young girls there were at and around these seaside resorts and all looking to be entertained or have some memories to take back home with them along with the seaside stick of rock. It was great to be young, confident and half-decent-looking. The world was my oyster. It still is.

Margate is buzzing and thriving, which is a bit of an improvement following a downturn like many holiday resorts around the country. Like Rhyl, Blackpool and other resorts, Margate went downhill, and the council stupidly allowed guest houses, hotels and apartments to allow the unemployed from around the country. Most of these, unable to survive in their own backyards, found it easy and inviting to go down and sign on the dole. When I worked there, it was still thriving, the bad times not far ahead, as hot sunny resorts like Benidorm in Spain started attracting more people with nice quality hotels that you could walk in and out of at will, unlike English hotels and guest houses where you were kicked out of after breakfast.

Flat and on the level, Margate, on the southeast coast, has plenty to offer the holidaymaker. On the Kent coast, the beach is long and sandy, with its arm stone pier, seaside stalls, fish-n-chips and seaside shore rides. The Turner contemporary international art gallery alone is worth a visit, beloved by JMW Turner and Tracey Emin. The Margate caves are another great place to visit where you can discover its history, including an iron age skeleton. Plus, the crab museum, yes, very interesting crabs. I found Margate one of the most attractive resorts to visit. Its only downfall to me in later years was its lack of accommodation for motorhomes, like most seaside resorts, unfortunately.

This part of the south coast Folkestone, Eastbourne, Hastings, Brighton, all along to Southampton, I considered cockney land for its obvious choice of destinations for the Londoners who come to this part of the south in their droves. The east coast, Skegness, and the west coast, like Wales and Weston-Super-Mare, are Brummie land destinations. Well, I suppose with some eight-plus million people living in London; they have to have somewhere to escape to. I think in Brighton alone, there are more cockneys than locals. Many like to drive down to their favourite resort, open up their little beach huts, set out the table and deck chairs and lord it over the locals.

Hastings, think of Hastings, and you think of 1066 and the Battle of Hastings because this is where it all took place. The Norman ruins of Hastings Castle, once home to William the Conqueror, overlooks the English Channel. The actual Battle of Hastings was fought in a nearby field where the battle abbey now stands. The clue is in the name. But there is more to Hastings than just the battle. Just along the seafront of Stade Beach sits the Hastings Fishermen's Museum and a shipwreck museum, which documents the maritime history of Hastings.

A modern rebuilt town with a new shopping centre, Hastings has suffered over the years and is slightly run down. With a long-level promenade and seafront stretching three miles, it has a pretty sandy beach. Sitting well back from the seafront on a mound, the remains of the castle command stunning views over the town and channel. In the late 1300s, the townspeople erected a defensive wall across the southern part of the town with three gates at the high street. The remnants are still visible today. As well as protecting the town from its enemies, it also resisted the sea from the strong southerly gales.

In the 14th century, during the Hundred Year War, the old town was twice attacked by the French, the second time leaving much of the town destroyed. George Street, which was originally known as the suburbs, was the first street to be built outside the town wall as it spread during the 18th century. Many of its buildings still retain their Georgian windows on their upper floors. To soak up Hastings history, wander around the old town with its tiny twittens or winding streets crammed with Tudor houses and flower-decked cottages, and inhale the hardworking fishing quarter with its towering net huts and ramshackle huts on the beach.

During this period, the town had a garrison of some 12,000 men led by the Duke of Wellington to help protect it from Napoleon Bonaparte. In Victorian times, part of the Bourne stream was covered and named Bourne Walk, and in the mid-60s, the town was completely split in two by the modern road. With its ancient churches and buildings' unique quarters, narrow streets (or twittens), and plenty of atmospheric pubs, shops and eating places, there is a timelessness about the town that we found fascinating. Hastings' old town lies in a valley between the east and west hills, each having its own funicular railway. Taking the east hill lift from the fishing beach up to Hastings Country Park gives you fascinating views from Beachy Head to Dungeness and as far as France.

The nature reserve covers 345 hectares and is one of three green flag parks in the town, the others being Alexander Park and the regency-style St Leonards Gardens. The west hill lift from George Street takes you up through a tunnel of rock to the ruins of Hastings Castle and the labyrinth of caverns with their history of smugglers, bootleggers and warring gangs.

In the centre of Hastings lies the American ground, a vibrant triangle formed when a great storm in 1287 threw up a silt and shingle spit beyond the boundaries of Hastings Borough. If you want something a little posher, carry on heading west to St Leonards, which was purpose-built in the 1800s by two brothers as a genteel resort for the aristocracy. How about that, then, with its architecture, art galleries, antique shops, chic boutiques and café culture, it still retains that same air of genteelness?

Another beautiful, exciting and diverse resort is Eastbourne. Just a few short miles along the coast from Hastings, with its long 19th-century pier and 1930s bandstand, an amazingly long pristine sandy beach, it has plenty to offer. All along the south coast from Margate to Bodmin, but excluding that far western tip down to Penzance is easy enough to reach and park up in the camper van. Even Dover had a couple of places to spend the night, that's if you've got the nerve to take that risk with all that lives in the town.

Speaking to a friend who had a relative who ran a pub in Dover, he told me what an unpleasant place it is to live, with most people being afraid to walk out at night with all the immigrants making their way into the port from wherever they came via boat, lorry or dinghy. Mind, after catching a ferry from the place many times, I'm at a loss to know why anyone would want to spend time there other than to catch the ferry. The town is run down and grotty. Driving along to the ferry port, you pass blocks of flats with balconies full of washing hanging from makeshift lines. Where is all the money going? The income from all the funds generated by the ferry companies, the fines imposed by customs and excise. I had to spend the night there once on the coast road opposite Dover Beach, my only comfort being the fact that it was so well lit I didn't feel bothered by the dodgy-looking flat opposite. The town itself didn't give me the best of vibes when I walked around looking for somewhere decent to find somewhere to eat. People walking about, shoulders hunched over, unsmiling faces. No, Dover is somewhere I book my ferry from, usually around midnight, arrive in plenty of time and on arrival in Calais, drive for at least two hours and 50 plus miles away.

Eastbourne, in contrast, is clean and tidy and carries an air of prosperity, most likely because of its proximity to London and its ability to offer holidaymakers what they want, plenty of good restaurants, cafes, chip shops, seafood stalls and pubs, and even more importantly, plenty of entertainment options. Contrast that with Dover, or Blackpool, famous for its lights, funfair and political gatherings, yet it's a dump.

First of all, you have Beachy Head, the, must see, geological nature and wildlife areas. The Birling Gap and the Seven Sisters a great places to spend the day with their two lighthouses and plenty of parking. The Eastbourne Miniature Railway and adventure park. Nature walks and several play areas. The Sovereign Harbour Marina is delightful with its choice of restaurants, walks along the boats and free parking. Whether that changes is debatable. The seafront is a pleasure to walk along, with fine sand and a flat-level sandy beach that seems to go on for miles with its beautiful Victorian hotels lining the front. Plenty of art galleries and the Devonshire Park Theatre for all those culture buffs. Fort Fun and the aqua park will keep the kids entertained for days on end.

Along to Seaford and Seaford nature reserve, then onto Newhaven, Saltdean to the next big town and a magnet for Londoners, I came up to Brighton.

Newhaven is a port town lying at the mouth of the River Ouse. The town developed from the middle ages as nearby Seaford began drying up. With its long curved shingle beach and chalk cliffs, it was a great place to spend a few days with plenty of places to spend a few nights in our motorhome, the only downside being its shingle beach. The positive side was it ensured peace and quiet. A sheltered harbour was built in the mid-16th century with a breakwater in the late 18th century. Newhaven increased in importance with the arrival of the railways in 1847 and cross-channel ferries to Dieppe. In circa 480, the Saxons invaded and established a village near Newhaven. During WW2, large numbers of Canadian troops were stationed here, and its ill-fated Dieppe raid was launched from its harbour. Lord Lucan's car was found here in 1974 after he vanished after killing his nanny, Sandra Rivet. The location suggested he had caught the cross-channel ferry, but no sighting was ever made of him.

Brighton is some 47 miles from London, hence its attraction to Londoners. Classified as a city, Brighton and Hove sit alongside each other in the county of East Sussex and date back to the bronze age and Anglo-Saxon periods. Brighton is a millionaires' playground with plenty of mega-rich residents, along with Russian oligarchs, city slickers and showbiz stars. It's high on the list of places favoured by millionaires, with its magnificent pier, big wheel, which gives fantastic views over the beach and town and, of course, the Royal Pavilion.

Brighton, home to Brightonians, is renowned for its quirky shopping areas and diverse culture, music and art scene. It has a large LGBTQIA+ community, which helps give it its title as the unofficial gay capital of England. Many people live here in preference to London because of its low prices and great access to the countryside and beachfront. Violent crime is one of the highest in the country, yet stars like Cate Blanchett moved to the city to start a family.

We spent a couple of days around Brighton, and the two things that stood out to me were the contrasts between those who had the money and those on minimum wage working in the place. With its unofficial LGBTQIA+ capital, it likes to see itself as a welcoming city which encourages many lesbian, gay, and bisexual residents. As well as its bohemian atmosphere, eco-friendly spirit and, of course, its Brighton and Hove Albion Football Club and the famous south downs. One in five is black or nonwhite, and some of the famous people who have lived on the western esplanade, often referred to as Millionaire's Row, are Adele, Heather Mills, Fatboy Slim and David Walliams.

Brighton is not a place that appealed to me at all. As well as the celebrities, it just seemed full of wide boys, chancers, villains and gangsters, including two of the most notorious landlords in the country. Running in parallel with them were the bottom dwellers, minimum wage earners and the unemployed trying to get a foot in the door working in the many restaurants, bars, and cafes around the city. Great, when you're in your late teens or early twenties, not so much fun, methinks, in your early forties or fifties. Maybe they might think differently.

ONWARDS AND UPWARDS

Heading northwest from Brighton, we wanted to spend a few days/nights over the South Downs. Home to the Blue Butterfly that thrives in the chalk grassland, Cissbury Ring is the second-largest hillfort in England. Covering some 1200 square miles, the South Downs National Park was only established in 2009 but has everything you need for glorious day trips or perfect holidays alike.

Famous for its rolling hills, ancient woodlands, chalk cliffs and unique market towns. It has something for everyone. We found plenty of places to park and enjoy walks and sights to see. Taking the A27 from Brighton, we leave the A27 at Chichester and head into the stunning countryside of Hampshire. Travelling through Hampshire and into the heart of the south downs to its highest point, black down. From here, you can visit Butser Ancient Farm or the iron age fort at Trundle. For one night, we stayed and had a meal at Ye Old George Inn in East Meon, but for the freedom, we found plenty of pleasant secluded places, although wild camping is not advised on the downs, like Dartmoor, I think, without permission. We had been told that this applies more to campers in tents, for obvious reasons. In our motorhome, we parked up and departed, just leaving our footprints. Full of cycle routes and paths, there are plenty of ways to enjoy the downs.

The South Downs Way is one of its most beautiful national trails running from Winchester to Eastbourne. It covers some

100 miles. But the downs have an irresistible collection of walks and attractions, from short breaks to long drawn-out walks (we gave those a miss), with its rolling downland, ancient woodland heaths and its patchwork quaint villages and towns that are each as pretty as the next. In those, we found the friendliness and welcome that was heart-warming, with good food aplenty.

From the South Downs, we made our way northwest and across, slowly, to Woolacombe in North Devon. Woolacombe, I'm really sorry to say, has never appealed to me except for maybe a day out. At over two miles long, the beach is fantastic, pristine, soft sand and faces the Atlantic at the mouth of the Bristol Channel and is faced by the Island of Lundy. With soft sand in the height of summer with the sun beating down, it's great. But that's about it unless you like travelling around and using it as a base. Or walking back and forth along the beach or seafront. Plus, there's hardly anywhere to park. Quite simply, the Devon Council, and probably many of its residents, don't want tourists. Well, they do, really; they need the tourists to spend their money. I know this from running various businesses in nearby Ilfracombe. We, the outsiders, are grockles. To park nearby, it's some 30-odd pence to pounds for a maximum of four hours. The beach is classed as the best in England and one of the top beaches in the world. But that's about it. Oh, not forgetting the surfing, of course. No. Mortehoe lying directly above Woolacombe, is only slightly better, with its rugged coastline and nearby Lee Bay. A calm cliff-top village listed in the doomsday book, it has spectacular views over Woolacombe Bay and beyond. Great for coastal walks along its rocky beach and cliffs. Great for a pint or a cream tea, ice cream or pasty, and the traditional fish-n-chips. Visit the Mortehoe Museum and get a glimpse of the days when smugglers lured ships onto the rocks down below. Told you they didn't like outsiders, didn't I? In the summer, they do tractor and trailer safaris out to Morte Point and Bull Point. From Morte Point

Atlantic, grey seals can be seen basking on the rocks or bobbing around in the sea on the north side of the point.

You can get a ferry from Ilfracombe or Bideford to Lundy Island, which is situated at the mouth of the Bristol Channel in the Atlantic, where there is one pub. Lundy is three miles long and just over half a mile wide. If you want to get away from it all, well, apart from 20-odd residents, this is the place to be or go to. No cars, no street lights. This is a place for peace and contemplation. Once a microstate, it had a few usurpers before the British Crown grabbed it for good. It is now a part of the Torridge District Council, North Devon.

Lundy is famous for its seabirds, including the puffin, which gave it its name. The Norse for puffin island is just Lundy, as no one adds 'island'. There is a wealth of other animals and plants on the island and the surrounding waters, including goats, rabbits, pigs, sheep, highland cattle and the famous Lundy ponies. The island includes a warden farmer, shopkeeper, bar and kitchen staff who run the Marisco tavern pub, all 28 people on average, who live in the village at the southern end of the island.

With no electricity, Lundy has its own generator, which is switched off at midnight (very basic here) except for the pub, which is all things to all people, so if you fancy a late-night stroll amongst the stars, make sure you bring a torch and don't get too close to the sea edge. There are 23 places to stay on Lundy, sleeping from one to twelve people, including a fisherman's chalet, lighthouse, converted pigsty, a late regency house and even a campsite. No, you can't take your motorhome over there, great as the idea might seem. The crossing takes about two hours, giving you four to six hours to explore the island. A world apart and surrounded by the clear waters of the Atlantic, Lundy is a haven for divers, climbers and birdwatchers.

Some years earlier, and when we had owned and run businesses in Ilfracombe, I had sailed my 32ft ketch over to Tenby in south Wales. After a lovely sail over, I made my way back after spending the night in Tenby Harbour. Not having visited Lundy, I called in for a visit. I wasn't an experienced sailor, and the Atlantic swell as I approached Lundy was some six feet and made it difficult for me to get up close for landing. Prudence made me decide to give it a miss and carry on to Ilfracombe. The only problem then was I lost my dinghy.

Now the dinghy was one of those little unsinkable things, so I turned around, threw my anchor onto it from the stern, grabbed it and hauled it aboard. I missed the first time around, then went around again, all the time navigating the 6ft swell, which in my mind was not growing to twenty feet. Each time I caught the dinghy, but I just couldn't heave it abroad or reach down to attach a rope. Trying yet again, I looked across to see a fishing trawler some half a mile to a mile away. Could they see me? Did they have a lookout? Looking down into the depths of that deep green swell, it suddenly occurred to me that maybe they couldn't see me. In fact, there was a distinct possibility that they couldn't see me. Realising my predicament, that if I fell in, in that swell, my chances of surviving or getting out were negligible. The odds of that trawler getting to me before I sunk into the depths were even more negligible. As my bottle went, I quickly abandoned the dinghy, worth some £40. The actions of my stupidity haunted me for some months after.

ILFRACOMBE AND NORTH DEVON

Appledore is a fascinating quaint fishing village with a maze of cobbled winding streets with the prettiest of pastel-coloured houses decorated with cheery hanging flower baskets and lobster pots. Situated at the mouths of the Taw and Torridge Rivers with views over to Instow, it is built on an ancient tradition of fishing and shipbuilding. You can wander past whitewashed former fishermen's cottages, which date back to the Elizabethan era. Appledore, along with Bideford, was at one time the biggest importer of tobacco and oozes tales of smugglers and secrets. Today the quay is central to life in the village, where you can enjoy a cruise up the estuary, a famous Hockings ice cream or even a bit of crabbing. Appledore is well worth visiting on a nice sandy beach with superb views.

At a fairly young age of late twenties, we took a week's holiday in North Devon. Seeing the brochure in the local post office window, we booked into the hotel advertised and run by Terry and his wife in Ilfracombe. Never having been to North Devon or Ilfracombe before, we were immediately captivated by its old Victorian charm and beauty. Surrounded by cliffs, Ilfracombe is a small seaside resort and harbour which stretches from the coastguard cottages in Hele Bay in the east to 4 miles along the Torr and to Lee Bay towards the west. Deceptive in its size, there are loads of things to do, from its little coves, trails, and little villages around the area. Leading down to the harbour along the seafront, you pass the famous tunnels, which are a private beach approached by four tunnels hand carved in the 1820s leading to sheltered beaches and a tidal pool, the theatre, which hosts some top acts and shows and hotels shops and amusement arcades to the opposite side plus the award-winning aquarium.

The harbour approached from two roads passing the medieval church is delightful. Small, it provides a safe haven for the local yachts and fisherman's boats that nestle there, protected from the harsh Atlantic gales. We fell in love with the place. Peaceful and laid back, it had, surprisingly, plenty of things to do to keep you occupied for a week or a fortnight.

I had made my living in the building trade till, inevitably, my back went. After lying in bed for two weeks in absolute agony, the specialist diagnosed I was suffering from a compressed lower disk. It was whilst contemplating my future working capacity that we took the week's holiday in Ilfracombe. Midway through the week, we observed that Terry, and his wife, were not very good cooks. In fairness, we were their only customers, and they were a friendly couple. They just couldn't cook. For breakfast, it was the traditional fry-up of bacon or sausage, beans, and eggs. The only thing fresh was the egg. Everything else was frozen, and you could tell. The evening meal was no different. Frozen chips and frozen fish in breadcrumbs with frozen peas. When you get fish in breadcrumbs, you always know it's frozen.

In life, you make decisions based on your knowledge and experience of how you lead your life. You hear of people who decide to buy a yacht and take their children sailing to far-flung corners of the world. That thought terrifies me. Then you have people who up sticks and take their children to live in different places around the world. Sometimes you have to question their motives. Were they genuinely thinking of their kids, the family as a whole, or just themselves?

I made the mistake of telling my wife during one evening meal, "Frozen food again," to which my wife replied, "I know." I then commented that I knew she could cook better, to which she made her second mistake of agreeing with me. Stupidly, I then remarked, why don't we run a hotel? She seemed up for the idea. The next day we went hotel viewing, and before the week was up, we had viewed a few hotels and even put an offer in on one right on the seafront; the offer was considered and accepted, and now we knew what our future held and where we were going.

Our plan was simple. We would buy a small, 17-bedroom hotel, my wife would do the cooking, and our oldest daughter would do the waitressing with all three of us mucking in on the chambering, cleaning etc., me running the bar. After five years, we would upgrade to a 25-bedroom hotel and, after another five years, to a 60-plus-bedroomed hotel. As I explained to our daughter Nicky, at that stage, she would upgrade to head waitress and my wife to oversee the cooking. Our younger children were either growing into the business or leading their own lives in whichever way they wanted to. Straightforward, really.

Our choice of hotel was spot on, near to the beach, harbour and Capstone Crescent. Our back garden overlooked the Bristol Channel. We had our very own swimming pool. Within 18 months, I bought our 32ft yacht, which I incorporated in our holiday brochure (enjoy a short fishing trip around the North Devon coast on our own 32ft yacht). It certainly helped fill our hotel up.

The one negativity that occurred to me was not the risk of sailing the yacht. The Bristol Channel had one of the highest tides in the world. At some 30ft, we could see the sea floor below us. At high tide, the sea rose to the top of the 40ft wall. In a force ten gale, well, let's just say it was awe-inspiring, but even that didn't put me off. But it did my wife, Bet. When she saw those waves, she decided never to sit on board. Oh no.

Not only did the yacht give me the opportunity to get out on the sea sailing, it also boosted the hotel bookings to no end. The holidaymakers loved the two or three hours of fishing, the bonus being to get to eat the fish they caught. Cod being first on my favourite list, trout and mackerel came a close second and third. Mackerel, a delicious fish, is one of the easiest fish to catch. Throw a line in, and almost immediately, a little group of Mackies will take the hook.

Often at regular intervals, I had noticed a large brown stain spreading out over hundreds of yards in the channel without giving it a thought till a bit of a "stink" was raised in the local papers. Quite a few people were upset that the Devon Council was dumping the raw, treated sewage into the channel at high tide, safe in the knowledge that the strong tide would soon whip it out to sea at 8mph. The thought horrified me. Not only did I enjoy aqua diving in the sea, but I also thought of the mackerel I had been enjoying. Coming or going up or down that channel, those fish would feed on that sewage for hours on end! From that moment on, I have never eaten another mackerel again. With its mild climate and ideal position, Ilfracombe had and still has a lot to offer. Yet it's a bit like Marmite. You either like it or hate it. I often wonder if it's maybe a bit of a culture clash with the locals versus the grockles who move into the town either to buy a business or just to live.

Dining options have increased over the last few years, with a varied choice of restaurants with even a Michelin star. Eat your heart out, Rick Stein. With a Damien Hirst Verity statue on the harbourfront, the town hosts a whole variety of events and festivals throughout the year, and there is always something happening, including the inevitable Morris dancers.

Along the coast to the east are Hele Bay and its working corn mill, with its watermill dating from 1525. You can even take home a cake made in the mill, and Combe Martin is famous for the longest main street in the country at some two miles.

Ilfracombe is a family resort simply because it has so much to offer everyone from the youngest up. From the beach to the harbour, the theatre and the Ilfracombe museum that holds treasures from around the world. Larkstone café and leisure park are perfect for a pleasant walk. One of the UK's most haunted houses, Chambercombe Manor, dating back to the 11th century, is another must-see. Other events are the food and music festival, the beer food and music festival, the maritime festival and the bike show in September. Our kids, along with the other kids, enjoyed jumping off the pier during the summer months into the cold, choppy sea. There are plenty of coastal walks along the southwest coast path from Hartland to Lynmouth. For gentler walks, take a stroll around Capstone Hill. Not far out of town, you have the Exmoor National Park.

Combe Martin, just along the coast, is another hidden gem with sandy beaches and secluded coves ideal for kayaking or paddling in a dinghy. For even more seclusion, you can head to Broadsands Beach either by kayak from Combe Martin or down its steep 250 steps. There is the Combe Martin Wildlife and Dinosaur Park with lifesized animatronics more like Jurassic Park. Just further down the road again is Watermouth Castle, overlooking Watermouth Cove with Merry Go Land and other fun attractions.

Nearby is the famous Pack of Cards pub, found halfway along the high street. Built in 1626 by George Ley of Marwood, it was built to celebrate a large win at cards and resembles a pack of cards with windows numbered to denote the numbers in a pack. To the east of the village, there are several derelict silver mine tunnels and the remains of a wheelhouse used to lift ore from the mine. Worked as long ago as medieval times, with activity dating back to 1292 with plenty of ties to the crown with part of the war expenses of Edward III and Henry V paid for with silver mined here. On the edge of the Exmoor national park, you have 268 square miles of walking routes of wonderful scenery and Exmoor Zoo. With its many quaint villages and country pubs or just strolling along the coastline, you will never get bored.

Lynton and Lynmouth, or little Switzerland as it is also known, lie a few miles along the coast in and around the villages of Lynton and Lynmouth. Reached by its cliff railway, still within the Exmoor national park, Lynton sits serenely on top of the cliff while Lynmouth sits at the river mouth below, the two connected by a heritage cliff railway. With plenty to see or do, it makes for an ideal break away from the bustle of life. Its harbour is small, peaceful and pretty, along with its promenade with plenty of cafes, bars and restaurants.

Lynton has a mix of independent shops, cafes and antiques along its many narrow streets, some of which are pedestrianised. The church of St Mary the Virgin is beautiful inside, with well-placed benches along the graveyard so you can sit and contemplate your future or views down to the beach and Lynmouth below. With plenty of delicious ice cream shops and cafes around the Lynton and Cliff railway. Within the oldest dwelling in Lynton is the Lyn and Exmoor museum, including photos from the Lynmouth flood of 1952, which wiped out much of the town. Rising 60ft, the West Lyn River carried boulders and debris down the valley and swept through the town's main street, many of the houses were destroyed, and 34 people lost their lives. The impact is still felt today. Caused by heavy rain during the previous two weeks, the situation was exacerbated by the narrow channel. It took six years to rebuild, and the river channel widened with an overflow to prevent it from happening again.

Another famous incident was the rescue of the ship Forest Hill in 1899, which got into trouble close to Lynmouth. Although the storm prevented a launch from Lynmouth, 20 men and horses dragged the 10-tonne lifeboat over the hill to Porlock Weir before launching the rescue bid. If that wasn't heroic, I don't know what would be.

A short drive from Lynton is the Lynton and Barnstaple Railway, a steam railway that has been restored as a visitor attraction, giving short two-mile rides from Woody Bay Station. A ride on the water-powered funicular railway is a must. It opened in 1890 and is fully powered by water. It's an ingenious feat of Victorian engineering with water from the Lyn filling the cars, allowing them to descend using only gravity. The journey up or down is thrilling, with fantastic views over the sea and harbour. For a change, you can walk the zig-zag path, which will do your heart a world of good. Either that or it will kill you. Another top thing to do is take a walk along the valley of the rocks with easy access from Lynmouth. Although a bit windy, there are plenty of stunning views. As a further bit of added useless information, Kate Bush, the famous singer, bought a house overlooking Lynmouth, where I gather her husband upset the locals a few times by riding a jet ski around the peaceful harbour. I don't think it helped that neither of them appeared to put themselves out to speak to the locals. Famous and not wanting to speak, tut.

The road leading us to our next destination, Minehead, took us over Porlock Hill. Most famous for its 1.4, Porlock Hill is one of the steepest hills on any main road in England. If you've got a big motorhome, my advice is to avoid it at all costs. Porlock Village is a beautiful picturesque village well worth a visit. One year, many years earlier, we had popped in to enjoy a coffee. The experience left me with an almost burnt-out clutch on my heavy Mercedes car.

Porlock Weir is the coastal village some 1.5 miles west of Porlock, with a long stone and pebble beach in a stunning location. The beach looks out across Porlock Bay. Both Porlock and Porlock Weir are worth a visit, with refreshments available. With an ageing population, just don't expect a busy nightlife. Porlock Ale in the famous Exmoor National Park enjoys picturesque moorland and rivers, along with its beautiful, rugged coastline. An ideal base for walkers, riders and cyclists alike with plenty of cosy pubs, nice restaurants, shops selling local produce and accommodation, including campsites

At some 500 square miles, Exmoor is one of the smallest national parks, but what it lacks in size, it makes up for in its beauty and history, with red deer and the famous Exmoor ponies, be amazed by dark skies and bright stars. With 1000s of miles of rights of way and high open moorland, it's a landscape that has attracted generations of poets, artists and writers. Doone Valley, made famous by Richard Blackmore, who wrote the novel Lorna Doone, has a lovely campsite that we used for a couple of nights before wild camping over the moors themselves. First published in 1869, Lorna Doone is the story of John Ridd, a farmer who finds love amid the religious and social turmoil of seventeenth-century England with Lorna Doone, part of the family clan that murdered his father when he was a boy. A staple in every school and library. Who has not heard of Lorna Doone?

Minehead, on the edge of the Exmoor National Park on one side, the Quantock Hills on the other, and the Bristol Channel on the other, is the area's largest town. It is also the starting point for the southwest coastal path stretching some 630 miles. Minehead is the perfect destination for a family seaside holiday. It boasts a lovely, long, flat sandy beach, a charming harbour, and a bustling town with plenty of shops, cafes and pubs. Nearby the seafront is Blenheim Gardens,

Mineheads largest park opened in 1925 and is open all year with a bandstand and a wide variety of free entertainment. St Michael's Church, built way back in the 14th century, and the cottages on North Hill add a bit of old-world charm to the town. Across from its promenade is West Somerset Railways, Western Railway. Opened in 1874 as the Minehead Railway.

Nearby are Watchet, Blue Anchor and Dunster. Minehead is also famous for its Butlins holiday camp with some 165 acres. Butlins opened in 1962, has something for everyone, and is accessible for the day to outsiders for a small charge. With its fair swimming pools and pubs, it can make a nice daytime destination. I must admit the Butlins Minehead is far superior to Skegness, with more space and better set-out rides. Clearly, Billy had learned from his early mistakes. Selected because of its flat ground, good rail links and closeness to the town and sea. The one problem Billy encountered was flooding, but he got around this by excavating a trench around the site and building an earth wall. The trench later became the boating pond. I told you Billy was sharp. Further attractions were added over the next few years, with the miniature railway, chairlifts and monorail. Two full-size locomotives were added in the early days, but these have since been removed and preserved.

With its Butlins camp, beautiful sandy beach, attractive town and proximity to Exmoor and many other attractions, Minehead is a great destination to aim for. In low season, we found plenty of places to park our motorhome without hindrance or upsetting anyone. Without a doubt, North Devon, Porlock, Lynmouth and Minehead are great, interesting and welcoming places to visit and stay.

The Blue Anchor village is a beautiful little resort set between Minehead and Watchet with its own train station, which houses its own museum of the West Somerset Steam Railway Trust. The village lies on the route of the West

Somerset coastal path. The coloured alabaster found in the cliffs gave the town its name, Watchet Blue. Also, the name of the pub in the town. Within the town is an old brick kiln built around 1830, which became obsolete in the 1870s when large-scale production started in Bridgewater. The town has a lovely long pebble and sand beach stretching all along the seafront towards Dunster with a long promenade where we could have camped up for the night whilst enjoying the village and the nearby Dunster Castle. Dunster Castle is a fascinating castle with plenty of rooms to visit, nice gardens to walk around and an interesting water mill. A truly fascinating place and a glimpse into a bygone era. Thankfully, the landlord of the Smugglers' Arms allowed us to stay in his car park free of charge with no obligation. My only regret is not having a coastal train ride whilst I was there. Another time, of course, hopefully.

Watchet, just further along and in North Somerset, is another hidden gem with a lot of history besides its pretty harbour and beach. The port was highly valued by Alfred the Great as he attempted to fend off those horrible Vikings. At one stage, it even had its own mint, producing coins. Before that, there was an iron age fort that is still evident today. The port came into its own again in the 19th century when iron ore from the nearby Brendon Hills was shipped to Wales. In 2000, the harbour was converted into a modern marina watched over on one side by the 150-year-old lighthouse and on another by the statue of the ancient mariner. The Quay itself makes for a pleasant walk with views across the Bristol Channel. There are plenty of other walks around Watchet, from long rambles along the Coleridge Way, the mineral line or shorter circular walks in the surrounding countryside.

The West Somerset Railway, brought here by Brunel, stops at the pretty station next to the marina and town centre. The market house museum covers the history of the town where kings, queens, murderers, knights, pirates, and saints tell their stories. The boat museum houses a collection of flat-bottomed boats. The town is packed with shops, restaurants and cafes, along with antique crafts and gifts.

Watchet has two beaches. To the east is Helwell Bay, rich in fossils and ammonites for the picking. West Street Beach has an old boating lake with amazing rock formations with quartz alabaster running through them and plentiful rock pools. We even spotted a Peregrine falcon and an egret. There are a couple of pleasant campsites nearby, but we spent a couple of nights around the marina with no problems at all. No one bothered us.

Along the coast heading back home, we called into Burnham-on-Sea and Bream. Burnham is famous for its low lighthouse built in 1832, grade II, listed with a red and white striped façade. Burnham was seriously affected by the Bristol Channel floods in 1607, so it has been busy reclaiming its land ever since, even building a concrete wall in 1988. There have been many shipwrecks on the gore sands because of their low depth. Originally a small fishing village, it grew in popularity as a seaside holiday resort in the late 18th century. With its low wooden pile lighthouse or the lighthouse on its legs, it makes an interesting backcloth to the long sandy beach.

Brean was a resort we drove into and virtually straight back out again after finding somewhere to park up, find somewhere to have a coffee and a burger. Brean is one big entertainment complex, very different from too many resorts we had visited, very geared up to the holidaymaker and making sure they spent every penny before they headed home exhausted and skint.

From one end of Brean to the other were holiday camps, campsites and amusement arcades, games and funfairs.

These types of resorts might appeal to many people. You don't have to think. Just pull up, get into your accommodation, and you are just led from one spend point to another, from one café to another cash machine. For want of trying something different, we booked in for one four days New Year's Eve break in Pontins, Brean. It was awful. The atmosphere was terrible, with a big percentage of the camp invaded by gipsies, who had all booked in separately. Never again.

Going off track a bit, we discovered a little pub just a few miles inland from Bridgewater and Brean called the Crown in Catcott. The Crown is a little country pub at the outer edge of the pretty little village. Surrounded by farmland and countryside, they have a very large car park that welcomes motorhomes and is quite popular. We first discovered it when someone commented on it in one of the camping forums we were on. They were singing the praises of its New Year's Eve entertainment.

Heading down there, we made it a bit of an extended break after the Christmas period, first having a day and night in a Weston-Super-Mare before heading across to the crown. The immediate attraction and niceness of the crown was its relaxed atmosphere. Closed when we pulled up. We just found a spot, parked up, and put the kettle on. There was no pressure to use the pub or facilities, which was the first benefit. It felt like no one was watching us. This was great for us because we are not great pub drinkers. Don't get me wrong, I'm happy to pay for and buy a couple of pints, but sitting in a boozer all night long supping pints is just not our scene. I grew up with it, a grotty little pub on every corner.

Likewise, with the food, especially the usual pub grub of frozen chips and tough frozen steak that can break teeth, the crown was very much different. The food was excellent, well portioned, simple and well cooked. As well as the steaks, they did excellent faggots and peas, steak n kidney puddings, liver and onions, which was more our taste. We eat to live, not live to eat. The prices were reasonable and the atmosphere friendly. With an open-log fire, you couldn't ask for more. For New Year's Eve, they had a live band, which made for a great night.

We haven't been down at other times, but if we were in the area, it's certainly a place I would call into for a couple of nights, a meal and a couple of pints. It's great to see more pubs welcoming campers, but it's unregulated, with pubs trying to find their way. First, campsites, to me, take the mick. £30 or £40 quid just to park up in a motorhome is just a push too far. Pubs are saying call in, park up for free, no electricity and no toilet facilities when closed, but then they explain that they just want you to have a drink or a meal. In itself, that's fine, but if there are two of you, a couple of drinks each can round up to ten or fifteen quid. Then a meal might be at least 10/12 or more pounds. That can be £40 or £50 for the night. For one night, if you want a meal and a drink, fine, but if the pub is in an ideal position, like alongside a picturesque canal with walks, and you want to spend a couple of nights, it can be quite expensive. Besides making you feel very conscious of the situation, feeling guilty, you feel obliged to spend.

PEMBROKE AND SOUTH WALES

In a straight line, it's close to thirty miles from, say, Ilfracombe to Swansea, longer than from Dover to Calais. Yet no one has come up with car ferry transport, that I know of, from one to the other. They have the people ferries, which seem to pop up when it suits them. You can get a ferry over to the Isle of Wight all day long, which is only about two miles. France has an abundance of ferries from Dover or other ports to the South of France, but to get to Swansea or South Wales from North Devon, you have to travel some 180 miles along B roads to the M5, then up to Bristol and onto the M4. Then back around. Pain in the backside at the best of times. So bad, in fact, that I would never have contemplated the idea. With the strong high tide in the Bristol Channel, I suppose it's too dangerous to consider a bridge. Certainly, I wouldn't fancy crossing it in a force ten, that's for sure, but a ferry? I am sure many people would be queuing up to visit the beautiful Devon coast from Wales and vice versa. Yet from Birmingham to Swansea, it's straightforward. Straight down the M5, onto the M50 past Worcester, then take up the M4. Easier, shorter and quicker than getting to Swansea from North Devon.

Shame, really, because surely both areas would benefit financially and economically if both doors are finally opened, which they surely must. There are some beautiful places in South Wales, like Tenby, Pembroke and mid-country, worth visiting. Because of the distance, we have always thought and gone in a more or less straight line. Well, onto the M6, then the M54 to Shrewsbury is the easy bit. It's from there that the marathon really begins. To break it, we've always tried to do Dolgellau, then Barmouth, through Wales from Barmouth to Pembroke. Or down the M5, then onto the M4. Some places need to be avoided at all costs, yet they can look quite deceptive. A place can look quite peaceful and ordinary during the daytime. One such place that springs to mind is around Lydney and Cinderford in the beautiful forest of dean. My daughter had treated me to a day trip on the Forest of Dean steam railway as a treat (somehow, she had picked up from my talks that I had once served as a fireman for British rail and trainee train driver). I decided it wasn't for me when diesel came in, and the old steam trains started rapidly dying out.

The thought was lovely, and I appreciated it, but you know, seen it, done it. Still, what could I say? Rachael dropped me off at the start of the steam train journey, where there was a vintage fair taking place. Rachael and my granddaughter had planned to find a campsite, set up the tent, and then come back and join me, by which time my train journey experience would be over, and we would enjoy the fun of the fair. We did.

At around six o'clock, we made our way into the local village, where we decided that a couple of drinks would round the day off well before retiring to the tent. Calling into the local spar shop, we got ourselves a bite to eat before hitting the pub. The village was typically rural and quaint, with an interesting stone feature. My immediate thought was, what a beautiful place to live, quiet, rural, peaceful, and friendly. Time to chat and pass a gentle hour. How wrong I was.

Hitting the first pub, we were told very abruptly not to come in. A bit surprised, we made our way to the next pub, where one of the two bouncers blocked our way and advised us to go elsewhere. Heading up to the top of the village, I opened the door to the last pub. Before I'd got the door open, the landlord shot over the bar, eyes wild and shouted to me to get out. Turning, we walked back down the village to the other far end. Now we were completely stunned, and I couldn't understand or believe what was going on. In the last pub, we walked into an empty side room where the landlord appeared, again shaking and wild-eyed. You can drink here only if you stop in this bar, obviously the snug, like he's doing me a big favour. We could drink here. The other side of the bar was loud and boisterous. Ordering our drinks, I couldn't help it. "What the hell is going on here?" Well, I used a more fruity language, of course.

Still wild-eyed, shaking and with fear in his eyes, he replied, "It's the drugs, mate. The town's full of it. Even my sons are into it all."

I was lost and couldn't believe what I was hearing. "If it's that bad, why stop here?" I said to my daughter. How desperate do you have to be to not get out of town?

Rachael lived in Bristol at the time and replied, "It's all over these areas, Dad. Especially the Forest of Dean and Gloucester." Sitting on the razor-ripped plastered seats, I could only wonder and sit in awe. What a dump. But this wasn't unique. Just one of the worst examples of it I have witnessed.

One downfall, or positive aspect of driving around the country, or Europe as I do, is you can cover a lot of areas and see a bigger and broader picture of what's going on than the normal holidaymaker or tourist, maybe even politicians who are only concerned about their own area and constituents. The fact is, we think we live in a free democracy where the truth is told on a daily basis, and nothing is hidden from us, nonsense. We are lied to every week.

During the mid-90s driving through Spain, we were looking at properties for sale. From part to full build. We assumed we were only looking at a few properties around Mojácar and the small local village of Turre till the solicitor, Rosario asked us how many apartments were available in the two blocks; I said three. When she replied 'no', I said, "I don't care, I only want one."

She replied, "But you must care because all of them are for sale, and if at least 50% is not sold, the utilities will not be switched on. A worse scenario is the entire block could be demolished."

But this was widespread all over Spain, worse on the coast and inland from north to south. You can see the joined-up thinking. First, the EU, Brussels, persuade Spain to join the euro. As an inducement, they offer them billions in bribes. Imagine these government ministers, "*Ay amigos*, what shall we do with all this money? I know, let's build a network of roads all over Spain in anticipation of all the tourists from Europe, Germany and England rushing to buy here." Every time we drove into Spain, we saw new roads being built. Many of the builders, with overconfidence that wasn't warranted, had persuaded the banks to lend them money hand over fist. Now the banks had snatched all the properties and land back and, with due prudence, were only allowing the properties to come on the market in drips. Quite sensible, really, in the circumstances.

But what about the drug problem in our country? Who's holding the truth back from us? How many of us think it's only our little village that has the problem? It's only because our young people have no work or recreation facilities? No one is joining the dots. We are then seeing the police nicking the odd major drug dealer or supplier and thinking, oh goody, goody, the police and government are doing their jobs. Nonsense drug taking is rife throughout the country, London, Birmingham, and every major city. Drug taking is a major part of life for many people. I don't think it helps that a lot of celebrities, pop stars, actors, business people, even politicians and the legal profession are stuffing it up their noses in abundance. In London alone, many a top party is noted for having silver trays on the table laden with coke. For the young, it must be very hard to say no. We all know it. We all hear about it. How can journalists catch a celebrity like singer Amy Winehouse, with blood coming out of her toes, apparently a known injecting point for hard drugs? If there is any truth in that, how come the cops were not there to nick her? I thought taking drugs was a criminal offence? Whatever the case, she is now dead.

We had decided to crisscross towards the south, calling into different towns or villages according to how we felt. One such place was Abergavenny, Blaenavon and the big pit museum. South to Barry, then along to Mumbles, Tenby, and Pembroke.

Abergavenny is a market town in Monmouthshire with lots of history. In the southeast corner of the Brecon Beacons national park and some four miles from the English border, it is considered or promoted as the gateway to South Wales, hence our visit to it. The town is a great base for walking, cycling and exploring. The town is a bit of a mecca for foodies, with gastro pubs, ancient inns and regular markets where you can buy locally grown produce. It has castles, mansions, Roman remains and standing stones. A bonus is the Monmouth and Brecon Canal. Not only is this a beautiful stretch of water, but it also has lots of places to park up with your motorhome to enjoy the peace and tranquillity. With the beautiful black mountains as a backdrop to the town, Abergavenny really makes a nice place as a base to stay and explore. With Raglan Castle just down the road and the world heritage centre at Blaenavon, there is plenty to see and do.

We stopped and viewed a pub between Abergavenny and the big pit. With a few acres of land and views over to the black mountains, we assumed it might be a good place to live and enjoy a good quality of life. We realised quickly it wouldn't be. The Brecon Beacons is a stunning, beautiful place to explore, camp up and spend a few days. The army and SAS use it as a training base.

My daughter Rachael had asked me to accompany her to complete her Duke of Edinburgh award by climbing the Horseshoe Mountain. It was embarrassing to watch men twice my age whizzing past me to climb to the top. Once on the top, it wasn't so bad once I'd got my second wind, but it was humbling, to say the least, on our final leg of the journey to watch soldiers on exercises running uphill towards us carrying full backpacks and not even breaking a sweat. Thankfully, Rachael gained her award.

The pub was owned and run by a cheerful-looking lady who had got the running of a pub well sussed out. Her only problem was she couldn't hide it. Having run a couple of pubs in Abergavenny, she had got a loan to buy this one. She also let us know she had formed a consortium with other publicans to buy their beer and spirits in bulk. Obviously, benefiting her. Knowing we were arriving to view, she had invited us to spend a few nights, which sounded and turned out to be a good idea. The land was plentiful but badly neglected; it had stables, which was a bonus, but it quickly became obvious that a lot of money was required to be spent on the land alone without the pub itself.

We had a brief drive around to get a feel for the area, and it also became obvious how deprived and run down a lot of the areas were. The big pit had once been a big mining work, employing people from the nearby towns and villages. These, in the main, had been built by the big coal barons who didn't give much thought to the miners themselves. Like soldiers, they were dispensable. The houses, or hovels, really were just quick and cheap knock-ups straight off the footpaths, so they could be woken or knocked up by the knocker uppers to ensure they were up and ready for work as required. It must have been dreadful and dangerous work.

The back gardens and well yards were just big enough for a brewhouse and line to hang the washing, like in Yorkshire and other mining towns. These men were employed to toil in the mines for low wages and were grateful for it. The only consolation was the free coal to keep their tiny houses warm. When the mines became unprofitable, the miners were thrown on the slack heap together with the rest of the slack. Knowing no better, their only alternative was the dole queue. To reduce the unemployment queue and make it look a little less embarrassing, someone must have given the nod to the doctors who started signing the men off with various ailments like nerve-related stress (which in all reality would have been true). Entire villages around the country were closed down without a thought to these guys' future apart from reducing the dole queue.

Driving around the place was depressing. Lord knows what it must have been like for those living there. The hardship and poverty oozed out of every brick and bit of render, the roads tidy but barren of people. Where were they? The thought didn't bear thinking about. I certainly didn't fancy popping into one of the pubs for a drink. To anyone looking, it was clear that it was going to take years before things improved. With that in mind, we drove back to the pub. Booking in for a meal that night, we were surprised at how quickly the restaurant filled up with customers. Hmmmm. Till we realised these must all have been friends or relatives rung around and brought in to impress us. They didn't. We progressed no further in our interest in the pub. Instead, we made an even bigger mistake and bought a pub and caravan site in Hereford. Duh.

Abergavenny, meaning the mouth of the River Gavenny, was originally the site of a Roman fort which became a medieval walled town within the Welsh marches, situated at the confluence of the River Usk and the Gavenny. Almost entirely surrounded by mountains and hills, including the nearby black mountains, the Marches Way and Brecon's Way, whilst Offa's Dyke passed through Pandy five miles to the north. There is a lot of history to Abergavenny, far more than I can cover in this book, but an interesting nougat of information that impressed me was the one about the Traitor's Gate.

One, Owain Glyndwr, attacked Abergavenny in 1404, and, according to legend, he gained access to the town with the aid of a local woman who sympathised with the rebellion. She let a small party in via the Market Street Gate at midnight. These could let a much bigger party in who then set fire to the town, plundering its churches and homes, leaving the castle intact. Market Street was referred to as Traitors' Gate thereafter.

Another interesting nugget of information and coincidence, the town grew from early Norman times under the protection of Baron Bergavenny, or Abergavenny. The first baron was Hamelin de Balun from Ballon, a small town with a castle in Maine, Anjou, France. He founded the benedict priory, now the Priory Church of St Mary, in the late 11th century. The Priory of St Mary lies in the medieval village of Lagrasse, a beautiful little village that I wrote about in my book "HAPPY CAMPING AROUND EUROPE," without realising or knowing about the connection. How about that? Two villages, hundreds of miles apart, in two different countries, and I had visited them both.

Merthyr Tydfil sits on the edge of the Brecon Beacons to the south. Local tradition holds that around 480 CE, a girl called Tydfil, daughter of a local chieftain named Brychan, was an early local convert to Christianity and was murdered by either

Welsh or Saxon pagans—uneducated non-Christians to you—she was buried in the town and considered a martyr after her death. Merthyr translates to Martyr in English, and tradition holds that when the town was formed, it was named after her. Merthyr Tydfil, get it? A church was eventually built on her burial site. I think the town has felt like martyrs ever since.

Spending a few hours around Merthyr, I couldn't help but feel how miserable people looked generally. I guessed this must be a throwback to its history of being a coal-mining and iron-making town. First, the Romans invaded and built a network of forts to merge their strength. The local tribes, the Silures, tried to resist but were outnumbered and beaten down. The Romans introduced Christianity before withdrawing and heading back to Rome. These were soon replaced by the Normans, with the Norman barons moving in after 1066. This resulted in conflicts between the barons and the sons of the princes with control of the land passing back and forth along the welsh marshes. No proper settlement was formed in Merthyr till well into the middle ages. People were being self-sufficient and living by farming and trading. This was until the ironworks and coal were discovered. In the early 1600s, the valley was almost entirely populated by shepherds, with farm produce being traded at several markets and fairs. It was the industrial revolution that completely changed the face of Merthyr, with its reserves of iron ore, coal, limestone timber and water. The demand for iron led to the rapid expansion of Merthyr iron operations. By the mid-1700s, the land was being leased for the smelting of iron ore to meet growing demand.

During the first few decades of the 19th century, the ironworks continued to expand, with at one stage 50,000 tonnes of rails leaving one work alone. Several railways linked the works with ports and other parts of Britain. Often sharing routes to allow access through the rugged country, which presented its own challenges. The world's first railway steam train, 'The Iron Horse,' pulled ten tonnes of iron with passengers on the new Merthyr tram road. This was claimed to be the first railway, with George Stephenson simply jumping onto the bandwagon and improving upon it. A replica sits in the museum in Swansea.

In 1802, Admiral Lord Nelson visited Merthyr to witness cannons being made for his ships. Thomas Carlyle, visiting Merthyr in 1850, wrote that the town was filled with such unguided, hard-worked, fierce and miserable-looking sons of Adam that he had never seen before. "Ahhh, me," he said, "it is like a vision of hell and will never leave me. The vision of these poor creatures broiling in sweat and dirt amid the furnaces and pits and rolling mills." China was the name given to the nineteenth-century slum in the storehouse area of Merthyr, mainly made up of English, Irish and Welsh. These were a separate class of people and were clearly visible by their lifestyle and appearance. No worse than some in Liverpool, Nottingham and Derby.

At least 1500 people were living in these slums, and the living conditions were some of the worst in the country. The slums, based around the narrow streets, were full of crowded houses that led to festering deceases. China became known as 'Little Hell', notorious for having no toilets, just open sewers, which caused diseases such as cholera and typhoid. More hardships came with the early 1800s with the sudden downturn in production, ruthless collection of debts, and regular wage reductions where some workers were paid in specially minted coins that could only be spent within the company's own shops. There were uprisings by the 10000s of workers marching and protesting with magistrates and ironmasters hiding under siege in the castle hotel. Soldiers were called in, with killings on both sides. One Richard Lewis was arrested and hanged for stabbing a soldier in the leg, although considered innocent to this day.

Following on into the 1920s and 30s, things only improved for the poor working class in Merthyr with the arrival of the Hoover company, who built a purpose-built factory for manufacturing the hoover washing machine and later the Sinclair C5. To me, it's indicative of how one man can treat his fellow men in order to make his fortune. And even now, as I walked around the town, I wasn't left with the feeling of great happiness. Those blacks working away in the old cotton fields of the deep south in America would have known what it was like to moan if they'd had a few stints down the mines or in those furnaces. Out of much hardship and suffering brings stories of success. The most famous are Howard Winstone, Jimmy Wilde, Johnny Owen and Eddie Thomas, not forgetting Joe Calzaghe. I think Joe is the only boxer you will ever see with a smile on his face. No, I'm afraid Merthyr isn't a town I wanted to spend a lot of time in.

My next destination before heading west to Tenby and Pembroke was Barry, just a short drive south. Barry is a little different from one or two of the mining towns in South Wales. For one thing, it's more prosperous. It is also home to Gavin and Stacey. Oh, come on, you know who Gavin and Stacey are. Barry is up and coming. Well, it has been for years for locals to visit for its sandy beaches and amenities, leafy parks, shopping and dining. Right in front of Barry Island is a huge crescent of golden sandy beach, great for families to enjoy the sun. Its promenade with its columned colonnade is full of busy cafes, amusement arcades and fish-n-chip shops. You can even hire a beach hut. Something you can't do on the south coast of England. Jackson bay is tucked around the corner towards Cardiff and, with no facilities, is quieter. On the other side is Cold Knap Bay. Well-named because of its position and pebbly beach, it's quiet, with plenty of space for windsurfing or a pleasant stroll along the promenade. At low tide, it has plenty of rock pools. Knap Lake and Gardens are ideal for a leafy stroll or a picnic overlooking the swans and ducks bobbing on the lake. Also a favourite spot for model boating.

Just around the headland is Porthkerry Country Park, with 220 acres of peaceful wood and meadowland crossing over the Victoria Viaduct. There's also a kids' play area, woodland walks, café, and picnic area, which leads down to the sea. Barry high street is a traditional high street with a traditional feel to it. Barry was famous for its shipping and dockyards, and a lot of its shops and restaurants are housed in repurposed fishing containers. Also, a Michelin-starred restaurant. Barry, once famous for its docks, was once the largest coal port in the world, serving all the coal mines in South Wales. St Barucs Chapel believed to be who Barry is named after, was built using Roman bricks and a Roman villa was discovered there. Barry was just a poor agricultural community until it developed as a coal port formed by a group of colliery owners who formed the Barry railway company, bringing the coal down from the South Wales valleys to the docks that grew rapidly. From one million tonnes in its first year to over nine million tonnes by 1903. The port was crowded with ships and had a flourishing ship repair yard.

The biggest exporter of coal in the world, its workers lived in terraced houses that rose behind the docks on steep roads overlooking Barry Island and the bay. At one stage, Barry Docks became one of the biggest repositories of steam engines, which were being replaced with diesel and electric power. It was the owners of those scrap yards that must take the credit for saving many of the refurbished steam trains saved from scrapping. Barry is still a port, with Barry docks forming the largest employment centre in the area, with direct access to the M4. With its first-class tidal position close to its deep-water channel, its ideally set to handle heavy tonnage with scheduled sailings with transit sheds, warehouses and open storage.

Barry Island Peninsula was an island until the 1880s when it was linked to the mainland. Now it is known for its amusements and Butlins holiday camp. If I'm truly honest, Barry came as a bit of a shock to me as I expected yet another dreary Welsh mining port and dreary dockyard. Barry and its surrounding parks, Victoria Viaduct and castle, were a revelation and a delight to discover. The only sadness is it's mainly a little gem only appreciated by the Welsh. The bonus was, for me, that there were plenty of places for us to berth up either along the front. Near the docks and in its car park, close to the town and its amenities. Certainly, it's a place I will visit again, mind. I like Wales anyway; I like the country of Wales, the countryside and its many seaside towns. It's just unfortunate that, like the English councils, our motorhomes ain't welcome so much as well.

ONWARDS AND WESTWARDS
TO PEMBROKE

I had wanted to bypass Porthcawl and Port Talbot whilst enjoying a nice leisurely drive along the coast to Mumbles, mainly because I'd heard the Mumbles area was a pleasant place to visit with a nice beach, friendly local pubs and, of course, the castle, Oystermouth Castle. It was just a 45-mile drive from Barry, but I was in no rush, calling into a little roadside café just outside Bridgend before making the final little push into the Mumbles. I wasn't disappointed.

The views from the Pier overlooking Port Talbot, Swansea, and the rest of the Welsh coast were stunning. It also has the Mumbles Hill local nature reserve, sited on the headlands on the western edge of Swansea. It says a lot that Catherine Zeta-Jones and her husband, Michael Douglas, have a home here, as does Bonnie Tyler, that husky-voiced singer who I think is lovely. I stuck it out for three days, hoping to see her, with no luck. One of the treats I enjoyed was the restaurants that served fresh food right off the boat. There is nothing I like better than a good portion of fresh cod and chips. You can tell frozen cod straight away because it dries up instead of having that wet, flaky fresh taste. It reached such a stage that I started to get fed up with asking fish-n-chip shops if their fish was fresh or frozen. It's very difficult for them to lie because they know it could be trading standards asking the question. Now I buy my own fish from the supermarket on delivery days and do my own fresh fish-n-chips in batter.

Mumbles Beach is small and sheltered with sand and rock pools between Swansea Bay Beach and Bracelet Bay. Safe enough for swimming in, it's a blue badge beach at high tide. The Norman castle, dating from the 12th century, has several events throughout the summer but closes in the winter months. We visited in the spring just as it was gearing up for the summer. The castle is impressive, but like a lot of castles in England and Wales, I often feel it might be nicer to restore them to their natural glory. Not all, obviously, Wales has a lot of castles, but I would have thought putting a roof on one could have made it more of an asset. Though at least Oystermouth puts on lots of events to celebrate and take advantage of the castle and grounds, which are not all that big. It only takes an hour to walk around it. The Mumbles it pretty and quiet. Easy to see why people would want to live there. The atmosphere is friendly, and we could park near the castle grounds, giving us simple walks into and around the pubs and town.

Walking into Swansea along the seafront made for an interesting day, the nicest of which was walking into the glass-roofed indoor market built in 1895 under the largest glass and wrought iron structure in the UK. It is stunning. Bombed during WWII, it was rebuilt and remains one of the most popular places today, with over 100 stalls. It has something for everyone. Including fresh cockles and laver bread, fresh cockles I love, so I was in my oil tot. The laverbread, made from seaweed and collected off the Gower shores, I gave a miss. Likewise, Swansea, the second biggest city in Wales and sits on the coast like most cities. I have to confess I am not a great fan. To me, cities are there to work or shop or maybe enjoy nightclubs. Swansea is famous for its nightlife, but for that, you have to have youth on your side. I don't. I find cities hard work. No, I prefer small villages or resorts where people slow down a few paces.

After a few days, two nice fresh seafood meals and three plates of cockles from the indoor market, I felt it was about time to move on to Pembroke, Tenby and the Pembroke Coast National Park. Tenby was just 60 miles around the coast from the Mumbles. Typically it turned out to be around a six-hour drive instead of the normal hour and a half or so under normal driving. Those Welsh might like to say they want us to visit, but they sure make it hard to get around. Famous for its medieval town walls and its beautiful beaches and old world seaside charm, the two main beaches are north and south at either end of the town, while the castle beach is nearest to the town centre and, of course, its castle. The remains of which sit on a promontory. Entry is free into the castle and well worth a visit. There are also plenty of public toilets and parking around Tenby, but in high season you can forget getting into the harbour area with a motorhome. I had tried it a few years earlier and had to carry on driving as soon as I got to the harbour entrance; it was bedlam.

Tenby is also famous for its beautiful coloured houses. Legend has it that the fishermen's forefathers painted them in pretty pastel colours so that they could recognise their homes as they were arriving back home from the sea. I would have liked to have caught a boat and visited Caldey Island, owned and run by a community of Cistercian monks, but it was just that difficult to gather the time to spend the required day or half day there. I managed to get into the shore car park, but that was about it. A few motorhomes have parked on the south shore with the tacit understanding of the council wardens, but that has been in low season. Again it's the mantra, go to a campsite or bugger off. Tenby is a place to be visited by car, stopping in one of the many guest houses. Shame for me because Tenby is one of the most beautiful little resorts in Wales. Its coastal path route has wonderful walks along the Pembroke coasts to Saundersfoot, with amazing views of Saundersfoot Bay.

Pembrokeshire covers the peninsular area from Tenby to Cardigan. All of it was beautiful and a bit more friendly to the motorhome owner. Mainly because it's got a fair bit of land to explore. Pembroke itself, together with its castle, has lots of history. It's also a place well worth visiting. Pembroke has lots of history, Pem, meaning head, and Bro, meaning region, country, or land, either lands' end or headland. The stone castle survived medieval times and was founded by the Normans in 1093. This stands at the western tip of the peninsular, surrounded by water on three sides. The seat of the powerful Earls of Pembroke was also the birthplace of King Henry VII of England. Following final extensions to the castle, in about 1254, the town was extended, and defensive perimeter walls were erected around the edge of the town. These walls were still on their medieval foundations. Many of the town's original Burgage plots survive and are divided by ancient stone walls.

Monkton Priory sat on a hill across the river from the castle and was founded in 1098 and granted to the Benedictine order. The choir and sanctuary were renovated in the 19th century, and Monkton Hall, close by the Priory Church, is considered the oldest domestic building in Pembrokeshire and possibly Wales. The first stone building in the town was the medieval chapel at 69a Main Street and built on the cliff edge. There are the remains of a great hall to the north, and the building was thought to have been used as an early church as the layout is the same as St Govan Chapel and used by John Wesley in 1764 to preach Methodism. In 1866, it became the brewery for the York Tavern, which was briefly Oliver Cromwell's headquarters at the end of the siege of Pembroke during the English civil war.

The town's main bridge across the River Pembroke, which also acts as a dam, crosses and constrains the millpond. The first bridge was built to house a tide mill originally granted to the Knights Templar in 1199. The last mill building was destroyed in 1956. There are still the remains of medieval and Elizabethan slipways where wooden vessels were built before the industrial dockyard was built. There is also a very early graving dock in what was Hancock's yard. The ferry port of Pembroke Dock is now three miles northwest of Pembroke and was established in 1814.

The town is centred on Main Street, which is the only street that is inside the original Pembroke town walls. The castle itself, at its highest point, is some 80ft high and overlooks the whole of the town as well as out to sea and along the coast for miles. The castle is stunning. The views are stunning. When we visited, we called into the Royal George, which sits directly below the castle. Me, my granddaughter, Bobbie and her son Riley. Whilst I'd got the time, I wanted my kids and their kids to see and experience a bit of our English history rather than just the usual funfairs and kids' entertainment draws. England, without a doubt, has a fantastic history and many historic buildings dating from medieval times. The motorhome provided a cheap way to see them.

We struck lucky by calling into the George for a meal and a drink and asking the very nice landlady where we could park up nearby for the night. Whilst we had parked in the castle car park, I never for one moment expected her to say park in the castle car park. It's not only free overnight. The warden never appears after 6pm. She was right. Parking up against the castle walls, we could enjoy a meal and a drink in total peace, apart from the odd cars that pulled in up to around midnight. After that, I didn't care too much. Right by the sea. Magical.

The area immediately around the castle itself, I felt, was a bit run down and poor looking, which is a bit of a shame and yet, I suppose, to be expected. No matter what part of the world we visit or have visited, it always strikes me that we are paying to see some architecture or attraction that is drawing tourists from around the world, yet the local community don't seem to see a bean.

Our famous Aston hall in Aston Birmingham is surrounded by Aston Villa Football Club and the slums. The newly or recently discovered city of Pompeii, well, some 50 years ago, is surrounded by run-down or slum housing. As are many historic monuments and buildings in Egypt. You would assume that any local government would have some pride and dignity. In presenting their town in a good light, in Pompeii, they must be taking millions in entrance fees and tours. Yes, ok, I appreciate it's an expensive job to restore and refurbish the city. Wages have to be paid, but who's drawing the rest of the money?

Pembroke Castle gave us a free tour, which was absolutely delightful and informative. I think even Riley found it interesting, which is unusual. The castle holds events throughout the year, culminating with a Christmas market in November with over 80 stalls featuring a mix of gifts, crafts, fashion and jewellery and a variety of quality foods and drinks. A celebration of the life of William Marshall, Earl of Pembroke, is held in May and June. Regarded as one of the greatest knights of the middle ages. There is the Merrymakers Knights' school, where you can dress up and take part in the procession. All are free with castle admission, so well worth a visit. There are lots of events like this throughout the year, but it's best to check before visiting. All in all, Pembroke was and is a delightful place to visit and stay, with plenty to do and see. Its beaches are clean and sandy and ideal for swimming, though cold even in summer. The locals were friendly and cheerful. You could feel the pride that people took in the town and its castle. An even better bonus is that there are quite a few places to park up in and around the area and spend a few nights, as with the Pembroke National Park.

With over 240 square miles and over 600 miles of public footpaths and bridleways, you won't get bored exploring and discovering the Pembroke National Park. There are over

200 circular walks, including half-day routes, gentle strolls, plus easy-access walks, most of them on flat-level ground. I must confess I must try to do more. I keep saying it and then making excuses. To be fair, being on my own, I don't find it as enjoyable as I should. I think part of the problem is twofold. The first is that finding anywhere welcoming around England or Wales is a bit of a revelation. I'm not used to it. I think you will find this applies to most motorhome owners. We're almost treated like lepers. 'You don't spend money' is their mantra. The last time I visited Barmouth, I got a ticket. I argued it and never heard no more, but what annoys me is Barmouth has some a mile along the seafront full of empty car parks for most of the year, and then they have the audacity to say we don't spend money.

Taking my grandkids, I spent over £350 over three days making sure they had a good time; we ate out mostly at the chip shop or cafes, plus spent a third at least on the funfair. I don't think that is mean. A guy opposite me also spent. How much, I don't know, but I saw him and his wife buy a few drinks in the pub. How many buy food from the local supermarket? Off-licence? It's still money, so it annoys me. Barmouth, in particular, has no foresight. They deserve to struggle. Tenby, I can understand a bit. In high season, it's small and compact, but Barmouth? Even if they set the far car park aside for us, it would be money earned. So no, apart from short two, three or four-day breaks, I prefer to spend most of my time abroad where we are treated differently. Parking areas are put aside all over France, where you would be hard-pressed to go five miles without finding an Aire.

So by the time I set off from home in Sutton to say Tenby or Pembroke, one or two days in each, I'm mentally closing down by the time I get to the national park. One night in Tenby, in low season, two nights in Pembroke, very nice too. Then here I am, over at the national park. I can understand the feeling at the height of the season, July and August, but for the rest of the time, they are hard-pressed to get over half full. Over the years, I have cut out places mentally that I know I can visit for one or two nights. Really, I should gear up to aim directly for Pembroke. Two nights around the castle, the rest over the park, hiking and enjoying the beauty of the rugged coastline. Yes, that's what I will do next time.

St Davids in Pembroke is the smallest city in Britain and has been a place of pilgrimage for centuries. The 12th-century St. David's Cathedral, built on the site of an even older religious building, is the reason for St David's city status. Tucked away in a sheltered vale beside the River Alun, the brooding gothic ruins of the Bishop's Palace lie on the opposite bank and give a backdrop to open-air theatre performances for which St Davids is known. St Davids is stunning, without a doubt. And the Oriel Y Parc galleries are a delightful place to enjoy a coffee and cake or sandwich.

You can take boat trips to Ramsey, Grassholm, Skomer and Skokholm Islands, where you can see plenty of sea life. Puffins, gannets, porpoises and dolphins, plus whales, to name just a few. St Davids was named after and founded by the saint David himself and was made a city in 1994 as part of the 40th anniversary of the Queen's accession to the throne, where it was decided that one city in either England or Wales would be given the honour. Wales won.

Fishguard, just around the coast a mere few miles, is only a small coastal town with some 5300 people, divided into two parts. It comprises the main town of Fishguard and the old harbour at the bottom of the steep hill. The surprising bonus is Fishguard has its own harbour train station. With its own ferry port, we spent a couple of very enjoyable nights down by the harbour where no one seemed to be bothered about us, and we enjoyed a delightful meal in the local harbour restaurant. With its rugged coastline and a pretty harbour,

Fishguard is a hidden gem, well worth visiting again and again. Preferably low season, methinks.

Cardigan Bay has everything you could wish for, a large inlet of the Irish sea indenting the west coast of Wales and the largest bay in Wales. A part market town, part holiday resort. It has the largest population of bottle-nosed dolphins. Take a dolphin spotting boat trip or a walk on the coastal path. Cardigan is a great family destination for a week or longer. With its castle in the centre, it is the most fascinating castle in Wales, with over 2000 years of history, from Roman times to the Norman conquest and even WWII. The castle has seen it all. The locals even have their own key, if you don't mind. With two lovely blue flag sandy beaches on either side of its jutting pier, we found a couple of places to park and enjoy a couple of days. Driving inland, we toured mountain lakes and waterfalls, market towns, and wild countryside.

We rounded off our break with a couple of nights in and around Tregaron and Lampeter, parking up in the rugby club car park. Tregaron is a tiny Welsh market town where the locals drive tractors, and muddy wellygogs are the norm. They start speaking Welsh as soon as they hear your English voice. Lampeter is a university town, and it shows, although still rural and Welsh country air, it is also very modern. I had stopped on some farmland up in the mountains outside Llanddewi Brefi, where I found a lovely little village with a pleasant, friendly village locals pub, till I made the silly mistake of saying '*yaki dah*' to the old boy next to me after he gave me a curt nod. He then started going at it, ten to the dozen in Welsh. Dumbfounded, and seeing my consternation, the landlady said something to him, "He's English," at which point he pulled a right face, turned on his heel and blanked me totally. Never say '*yaki dah*' to an old Welsh boy in Wales.

THE DERBY DALES
VILLAGES AND TOWNS

Ahhh, the Dales. Just the names conjure up rustic excitement, nature, wilderness mountain and hill climbing, exploring and canoeing, the Dales, Darley Dale, Two Dales, Darley Bridge, Snake Pass, Matlock Bath and Stanton in the Peak. Peace, tranquillity, and a feeling of being at one with the ground beneath your feet.

We had been visiting the Dales for years, right up into the Yorkshire Dales, and never tired of them. The rivers, streams, mountains and lakes, as well as the little towns and villages that were dotted around the counties as they had done before medieval times. There is something permanent about the Dales. Visit tomorrow, and you will see the same bridge, village stream or river you visited twenty years ago, except for maybe the local village pub. That may have disappeared in the name of progress and inevitability, i.e., lack of use. Those that survive are the ones that can provide good food. The rest will be converted into nice little country cottages or village houses.

Not quite into the Dales, but just as interesting is Ironbridge. A large village in the borough of Telford and Wrekin in Shropshire, located on the banks over the River Severn at the heart of the Ironbridge Gorge. It lies in the Gorge that Ironbridge developed beside and takes its name from the iron bridge. 100 feet long, the cast iron bridge was built in 1779. Promoted and known as a tourist destination, it's also considered the birthplace of the industrial revolution. This was because of Abraham Derby; see that Derby again? Perfected the technique of smelting iron with coke in Coalbrookdale. This allowed for much cheaper iron. The industrial revolution didn't just start here, though. Oh no, but the bridge, being the first of its kind made from cast iron and one of the very few to have survived, remains an important, poignant symbol of the dawn of the Industrial Revolution. 1779? We were still living in mud huts and were only just leaving the medieval period. What a fantastic achievement. It was Abraham Darby III's grandson that built the bridge, designed by Thomas Farrols Pritchard, to link the two areas, and it took three years to complete finishing on New Year's Day 1781.

Soon afterwards, the ancient Madeley Market was relocated to the Square and Butter Cross, formally being renamed and becoming Ironbridge. The same people who built the bridge then built the Tontine Hotel. Across the square and facing the hotel stands the war memorial erected in 1924. A bronze statue of a First World War soldier, sculpted by Arthur George Walker and erected by A. B. Burton. Above the river is situated the 16th-century hunting lodge with many of the 17th and 18th-century workers' cottages. Together with some imposing Georgian houses built by ironmasters and river barge owners. Amongst those are various Victorian villas built using locally coloured bricks and tiles from around the locality.

St Luke's Church, built in 1837, is unusual in design in that its sanctuary is at the west end and the tower at the east, in reverse order to most of the churches. This is because the land at the west end was unstable and unable to take the weight of the tower. The bells were installed in 1920 in memory of the locals who died in WWI. The external clock was illuminated in memory of those who died in WWII. As a little titbit, Ironbridge is also the birthplace of the England national football team captain Billy Wright.

By the 19th century, the settlement started to go into decline, but in 1986 it became a world heritage site. Covering the wider gorge area, it became a major tourist attraction for most industries, being tourist related with a small museum for the Merrythought Teddy Bear company established in 1930, together with shops, various pubs, cafes, and small shops. The fish-n-chip shop situated close to the statue is a favourite with visitors, us included and was well worth the wait in the queue. The Queen visited and had a walk over the bridge in 2003, and the annual Coracle Regatta is held on the River Severn, along with many others throughout the year. Mainly because the Coracle-making family of Rogers lived in Ironbridge for several generations.

Ironbridge, central for many visitors, makes for a very pleasant and interesting day out. Once you cross that bridge, it's like stepping back in time. In fact, I'm always surprised that the locals are not walking around in Georgian or even Edwardian clothing. Because that's how it feels, a lovely ambience, much like a visit to the Black Country Museum.

Matlock Bath is another favourite for many Midlanders around the country, tourists, day trippers and bikers. Why bikers, I often wonder, but there they get, lined up along either side of the road, admiring each other's steeds as they lean back and enjoy a pint. Or maybe not. Matlock Bath, or Matlock By Sea, as some people view it, because for many of us it's like a day out at the seaside, much like Stourport to us Brummies' or Black Country folks.

Lying in the peak district south of Matlock town on the main A6, around the River Derwent and about halfway to Buxton and Derby, the village only holds about 750 people, but it swells with the tourists. It was developed in the 19th century as a residential and spa town. The steep hillside on the one side of the river prevents any building or development, with most of the buildings, shops and attractions all on the one side. The early coaching road that led over the very steep hills was replaced with the straight-through road of the A6. In 1698, warm springs were discovered, and a bathhouse was built as the waters became better known and access improved with a bridge into Old Matlock. Princess Victoria's Royal visit in 1832 confirmed Matlock as a society venue of the time, a little more upmarket than Stourport-on-Severn then. Victoria's party visited a pair of museums and a petrifying well. John Ruskin and Lord Byron were visitors and compared the place with Alpine Switzerland, leading to its nickname of Little Switzerland. Erasmus Darwin recommended the area to Josiah Wedgwood for its beauty and soothing waters, and members of his family settled there. Edward Levett Darwin, son of Francis, lived at Dale House in Matlock, where he was a solicitor. At the far end of town, the railway station opened in 1849, with Beaching making his cuts in 1968. Now it runs daily from Matlock to Derby on the Derwent Valley Line, with carriages plying for hire. Matlock Bath is a designated conservation area with Article four directions in relation to properties along the north and south parade.

Major attractions include the heights of Abraham Park, Gulliver's Kingdom Theme Park and the Peak District Lead Mining Museum. On the opposite bank of the River Derwent lies high tor, a sheer cliff used by walkers and climbers alike. It also features Giddy Edge, a narrow winding path along the cliff edge, a nerve-racking walk if you're afraid of heights. I dislike heights. Much more attractive is the circular walk along the river on the town side, crossing over the bridge and along the lover's walk along the cliff edge to the second bridge further down. It makes an attractive walk at whatever time of the day, with plenty of distractions along the way.

The heights of Abraham Cable Car link the base of High Tor rising to the Heights of Abraham. In the autumn of each year, the Venetian Nights are held with illuminations along the river and illuminated boats, at some only 50 miles from me in Sutton. It's well worth the visit just for that alone. Many years ago, when the children were young, we threw a comb into the petrifying well. Going back years later, we could never find it or see it. When we first started visiting in our motorhome, we could park at the far end of the town between the railway station and the end pub. The car park was discreetly tucked away out of sight and stretched for some distance. I don't know if many people knew about it as it was and is tucked away, but at the time, there were two or three other motorhomes there. The last time I went, which was just recently, the car park was totally empty and signs up saying no overnight camping. This really makes me pull my hair out. Has anyone taken the liberty and damaged things for the rest of us? I wonder. I know there are some campers who give no thought or consideration to the rest of us coming after, like dumping rubbish or worse without seeming to realise or have the brains to appreciate that they have just really buggered it up for themselves the following years.

I also wonder if a lot of the smaller vans with no toilet or other facilities on board are responsible. I mean, if there are two or three on board, where do they go? At any rate, I then discovered the railway station car park, which stretches right back and along the line. I wasn't too bothered about the noise from the train, but I went back to the original car park, up to the far end, and tucked myself into some bushes. Oh well, the car park was empty, and I was only stopping the night. I might well have stopped another night or two for the sake of a simple parking ticket. A shame, really, because some restaurants along the road offer excellent service and surprisingly good fish and chips at a reasonable price.

Matlock, a short drive north, is a bigger town that also has plenty to see and do. Crown Square and the River Derwent lie at the heart of Matlock and the gateway to Hall Leys Park. With its boating lake, riverside walks and Hall Leys Park, one of five beautifully restored parks to Matlock Bath. With plenty of shops, restaurants and antique shops, Matlock makes a pleasant contrast to Matlock Bath.

Nearby villages are Darley Dale, centred around its church and near the River Derwent. The village owes much to Sir Joseph Whitworth, a wealthy industrialist who lived at Stancliffe Hall. In the churchyard is an old yew tree with a girth of some 33ft and is one of the thickest in the country. Across the river from Darley Bridge is Oker Hill, which gives a fine vantage point to view the Derwent Valley.

Riber is a small medieval hilltop hamlet overlooked by the imposing shell of Riber Castle. Local entrepreneur John Smedley had the castle built, and it has been a landmark for miles around since 1862.

Two Dales is another Hamlet whose name comes from the two valleys of Hall Dale and Sydnope Dale run on either side of the village. Once known as Toad Hole—don't ask—Two Dales was a thriving community which first produced flax and then lace, then animal feed. The mill was water powered by the three reservoirs lying in the valley and gives pleasant walks through quiet woods.

Ashbourne is one of the nicest towns in the Dales area, northeast of Alton Towers and south of Matlock Bath and Bakewell. It is known as the gateway to Dovedale, and I think that is probably an apt description. Only a short drive from Sutton Coldfield. I never tire of visiting the place, and each time I visit, I never fail to see something different. My only criticism is the lack of parking for motorhomes. There are two or three free parking areas around the town centre, for cars, some, like the supermarket car parks, are free for two or three hours.

The one main car park in the centre has twenty-four-hour parking, so once or twice I've been a bit cheeky and parked up overnight. Well, it does say free twenty-four-hour parking. With its winding cobbled streets welcoming marketplace and handsome Tudor and Georgian heritage, Tudor, Georgian and Victorian buildings are bountiful around the town. Without a doubt, it's the perfect base if you want to explore the spectacular limestone landscapes of the Southern White Peak and nearby villages, towns and Dales. Alton Towers is nearby, Chatsworth House a short drive away, as is Haddon Hall, Matlock, Bakewell and Buxton, plus lots more.

If I died and went to heaven, I couldn't ask for anything nicer than to set out from home and call into Cannock Chase for a couple of nights. The forestry commissions Tackaroo site, then a night by the canal at Fradley, with a meal in the local pub followed by a steady drive to Ashbourne and a few days here, bliss.

With over 200 listed buildings, including the historic Alms-House's Fine Coaching Inns and genteel townhouses, Ashbourne really is a visual feast for the visitor. My first port of call, having parked up discreetly somewhere in the car park, is the nearest coffee shop, just a short walk through the first narrow streets, past the supermarket, soaking up the atmosphere as I go. Everything is at a slower pace. After an hour of just people-watching and enjoying the ambience, I then set off along the narrow alleyway into the main street, where I'll do a right along and towards the market square. On the square itself is a very nice fish-n-chip shop where I try to have an afternoon or early evening meal.

Spreading across St. Johns Street is the biggest Gallows Inn sign in the world outside the Green Man Pub and Black Boy Head. Originally it had a figure of a black boy's head above the centre, but this was taken down as we became more politically correct and woke. I can take a short stroll around the town centre with all its vintage and historic shops selling local delicacies, antiques, food and drink, all in individual little shops of character. Taking the road out of town brings me past more fascinating antique shops before coming to the façade of the grade I listed grammar school. A little further on is St Oswald's Parish Church, with its 212-foot high spire described by author George Eliot as the finest single spire in England. Walking around the church is, I found, humbling and thought-provoking.

The much-boasted Ashbourne gingerbread is, in fact, not the Ashbourne invention. During the Napoleonic wars in 1799—1815, French prisoners were kept in the town. One prisoner was the personal chef of a captured French general. Who was kind enough to share the original recipe with the locals? It had nothing to do with any threats, like 'Give us the recipe, or we will chop your head off'. The timber-framed gingerbread shop can still be seen on St John Street, and the original Ashbourne gingerbread can still be purchased in the town. Shopping is a real pleasure with its many small shops, family-run businesses and weekly open-air market, held in the cobbled market square every Thursday and Saturday. This was given a Royal Charter in 1257. Before relaxing over a coffee, lunch or afternoon tea, all served with a relaxed attitude, almost indifferent. Also famous for its ancient tradition of Royal Shrovetide Football, started by such luminaries as Prince Charles Stanley Matthews and the Duke of Devonshire, who played each Shrove Tuesday and Ash Wednesday. An event that bears little resemblance to the modern game, of course. With its unique and unruly behaviour.

The town also sits on the famous Tissington trail, the green gateway to the Dovedale and Pennine Bridleway linking up further north with the high peak trail. Commencing in the town, it starts with a Victorian tunnel about 380 yards from the site of the former railway station. It follows the course of the railway through the village of Tissington and joins the high peak trail, a bridleway, a footpath and a cycleway. It stretches some 13 miles; I did about three. In medieval times, it was a frequent rest stop for pilgrims walking the St Nons Way to the shrine of Saint Fremund at Dunstable. The forces of Charles Stuart also passed through the town during the Jacobite rising of 1745. Henmore Brook, a tributary of the River Dove, flows through the lower middle of the town and makes yet another pleasant area to sit and relax. In 1881, four gentlemen of the town founded a society aimed at improving the standard of Shire Horses in and around Ashbourne, originally called the Ashbourne cart horse society. It held its first show in the paddock. It was so successful it became permanent. An annual show has been held ever since royal patronage was granted in 1899 by King Edward VII, who was president in 1901. It has grown and evolved, with cattle being introduced in 1925 and sheep later.

Ashbourne has eleven public houses, the most famous being the Green Man and Blacks Head Royal Hotel, which closed and underwent a change of ownership before reopening. The rare gallows sign across St. Johns Street became the focus of a racial debate with its caricature of the black boy's head atop the sign. It was removed after a petition gathered over forty thousand signatures. Considering there are only about eight thousand residents in the town, I wonder where they all came from. At any rate, it is a favourite meeting point in the town. I can imagine how it must have been. "Ok, John, we'll see you under the black boy's head on Friday."

They say variety is the spice of life, and without a doubt, there is plenty of variety within a short distance of Ashbourne north, south, east or west. To the southwest of Ashbourne are Alton and the famous Alton Towers. This is a complete contrast to Ashbourne and the surrounding areas, with plenty enough to keep you occupied for a day or two. In contrast, you might need another day or two at Ilan to recuperate after the experience. With over 500 acres of grounds set within the beautiful Staffordshire countryside, three themed hotels, plus over 40 world-class rides and attractions like the heart-pounding roller coasters, Wicker Man and Oblivion, without a doubt, this is one of the best theme parks in the country and plenty enough to keep you occupied, people return year after year.

Ilam, just 5 miles northwest of Ashbourne, is the most famous for its neo-gothic Ilan Hall, built originally in the 15th century by the Sir John Port family. Sold after many years because of financial difficulties. It then became home to the

Russell Watts family. Now, it is a famous YMCA hostel run and owned by the national trust. Its shop and tea rooms are open daily and free to national trust members. Ilam is famous for its natural beauty, scenery and landscape, an excellent getaway from Alton Towers and city life. We happened to just be driving through it when we came across a little discreet sign saying camping. After enquiring with the local farmer, we pitched up in his field with the River Manifold adjoining. With no facilities except water, milk and eggs from the farmer, we had two nights of utter bliss. No sounds other than the natural sounds of the night, with owls and other creatures foraging for food, the stars shining bright in the night sky.

For another spell of utter peace and quiet, you have the Nine Ladies less than twenty miles away. I had never heard of the Nine Ladies, never mind who they were or what they did. Whilst we were meandering around the Dales, a friend insisted we must visit the Nine Ladies whilst we were in the area. The Nine Ladies is situated on Stanton Moor, Stanton in Peak, a place worthy of a visit in its own right. This is an early bronze age stone circle believed to depict nine ladies who were turned to stone as a penalty for dancing on a Sunday. In those days, the ladies had a tendency to go up on the moors dancing alone and under the moonlight; it is part of a complex of prehistoric circles and standing stones on Stanton moor.

Managed by the Peak District National Park Authority, camping is absolutely prohibited on the moor, with the roads adjacent to Stanton Moor being so narrow and very difficult to park on, making it difficult to access the site. However, this didn't stop the different cars from finding somewhere on the banks to tuck in and park up, including me, where I spent the first night directly opposite the footpaths, which is the starting point for the ladies themselves. The surface leading to the stones is rough and uneven and totally unsuitable for anyone with any disabilities or walking problems. Passing through fields and woodland with gates and stiles, I found it difficult enough as it was. From the roadside, the walk was some three-quarters of a mile to the stones, which were, as described, set in a large stone circle set in open ground. Even in the low season, there were plenty of people there from all over the country when I visited. There were different circles of walks to and around the site, including a small circular walk from the roadside, which goes around the stones and then returns. There are larger circular walks, which go further with other walks leading off in different directions across the moors. For hikers, this was a dream place to visit and explore.

Although the rules on camping are very strict, well, I didn't see many signs of who is monitoring it. I saw no one. No rangers, no wardens. Around the stones themselves, people were relaxing and enjoying the day, spread out and in groups, either in twos or families. Most of the people I saw were obviously hikers walking across the moors, but I also noticed people hidden away amongst the trees in tents and next to campfires. I was half tempted to walk across around midnight to see what, if anything, was going on. But I thought better of it. Well, you don't know what weirdos are up there, do you? Like most people, I have heard enough strange stories of cult followers or leaders getting together, performing rituals that don't bear thinking about, moon worshipping, sun god worshipping, and god knows what else worshipping. No, thank you. I enjoyed the night under the stars on a nearby embankment with my door open, overlooking the fields under the night sky. My first twenty-four hours were so enjoyable I spent another night there. Stanton Moor and the Nine Ladies, with their accompanying hiking trails, are somewhere you can visit again and again.

Just a short walk away were a couple of pubs, so I thought I might head into one, park my motorhome and have a meal. I considered asking if I could park overnight but, on reflection, realised that I felt quite safe and undisturbed by the side of the road. After seven pm, the traffic dropped to the odd car coming past and after midnight, that dropped to zero. Locals in this part of the world are tucked up well before midnight, and visitors have long gone home. The only ones around were those who, for whatever reason, were hiding up amongst the stones and keeping discreet. Parking is available about a mile from the circle and consists of a large section of ground set aside for that purpose. I considered spending the second night on it but felt quite comfortable with where I was. Nearby are two other prehistoric sites in the care of the Peak District National Park. Arbour Low, a Neolithic Henge, is six miles away, and Hob Hurst's House, a burial chamber, is three miles to the northeast.

You will enjoy beautiful peak district views from each. There are also the imposing ruins of Peveril Castle on a hillside overlooking the village of Castleton and offering breathtaking views across the hope valley and beyond. Nine miles away are the remains of the once-beautiful Wingfield Manor.

The vast and immensely impressive palatial medieval manor house, arranged around a pair of courtyards, Wingfield Manor was built in the 1440s for the very wealthy Ralph, Lord Cromwell, treasurer of England. It was later the home of the husband of Bess of Hardwick, the Earl of Shrewsbury, imprisoned by Mary, Queen of Scots. Wingfield Manor is open at various times of the year, but it is part of a working farm, so discretion and respect are called for.

I have considered joining the national trust, which gives unlimited access to these treasures, but the problem I find is where do I park? I don't want to go to nearby sites when I am totally self-contained. At one stage, I kept hearing that the trust was going to set parking places aside for motorhomes and if this was the case, it would be absolutely great, so long as it was a reasonable fee. This would mean being able to park up, view the property, and then sit back without any pressure and look back at the day or view the next day. This is quite common abroad, especially in France. But here, it's very money orientated. Thankfully, there are quite a few places still to see in England where you can feel the freedom whistling around your ears without being hassled by some jobsworth in a cap. That's in the country. Here in the Peak District, there are lots of places. The Peak District, right on our doorstep, means getting back in touch with nature.

The Peak District was, in fact, our first national park created in England and Wales in 1951, probably because of the Kinder Scout mass trespass in 1932, where some 500 walkers made a mass protest for the right to walk. One of the starting points for this trespass was the village of Hayfield, an absolutely beautiful little village beauty spot in the Derbyshire countryside.

From here, we enjoyed a nice circular walk that took us up to the moorland, giving us magnificent views over Kinder Reservoir. After the walk, we enjoyed a pint and a nice meal at the Pack Horse Inn in Hayfield itself. This is a five-mile circular walk from the Bowden Bridge car park and follows the Kinder Road towards Hayfield, turning right for Snake Pass.

Leading you uphill (a bit of a steep climb), we passed the Kissing Gate, a copse known as the twenty trees. Sticking with the snake path, we then reached the moorland and a white shooting cabin on the left. Follow the path signposted by the Snake Inn and

Edale, and take the track to the left, giving amazing views of Kinder Reservoir. Snake Inn itself is yet another place with a friendly landlady who allowed us to park up overnight. Keeping the reservoir to your right, follow the path to William Clough and a small bridge crossing the stream. Past the pine trees and a walled pine plantation before eventually descending through a field towards the trees and stream. The path took us on towards the trees and stream, then on towards Hayfield. Done in and crackered, we enjoyed that delightful meal and a pint. Further along on Kinder Road is the Sporting Inn, a traditional country pub with a cosy atmosphere and a roaring fire. We had another pint there as well. Well, we had walked a few miles.

Another favourite place that I enjoy visiting every time I visit the Dales is Bakewell, the home of the famous Bakewell Tart. Like many of the small towns and villages around the Dales, Bakewell has a lot of history. Pulling in by the cattle market, there are plenty of spaces on the opposite side of the track/road, which seems to be acceptable for motorhomes. Whilst the parking spaces nearest the market have parking spaces, they are for cars and clearly not motorhomes. At any rate, that's how I saw it and parked up amongst other motorhomes who felt the same. On market days on a Monday, the cattle market itself is a hive of excitement and activity, with a decent café selling reasonably priced food. Walking past the market, I headed straight for the bridge leading over the River Wye and into the main town. For some reason, the bridge itself has become a magnet for young lovers, leaving their little locks on the bridge with their initials swearing lifelong love and devotion. Who came out with this lovely great idea? I don't know, but I witnessed it on the Bridge of Sighs in Venice. The only problem was the council had to put a stop to it. I understand because the ancient bridge weighed down with tons of locks, was in danger of sinking. I wonder if Bakewell Council will eventually do the same thing? Some locals are having a little moan. Personally, I thought it added to the prettiness and romance of the town.

There is a lovely circular walk of about five/six miles along the river from the bridge, which takes you along the banks of the River Wye into the picture-perfect village of Ashford-In–The–Water, from there it heads up onto the Monsal trail before returning on quiet field paths back to Bakewell.

Whilst in Ashford–In–The–Water, only two miles along the river, we stopped for a walk around the village. Named after the ash trees that grow in the village, In–The–Water was added years later because of its proximity to the river. In 1786 Ashford had Mills that carved and polished the local black marble for which it was famous. Also, the Maidens' Gardens were created to mark the deaths of the virgins in the village (this was a practice that carried on until 1801 when presumably no more virgins existed there). The tradition of the Well Dressing still survives today, where village volunteers decorate the six wells in the town, marked by a procession through the town.

Although an earlier settlement, Bakewell was probably founded in Anglo-Saxon times in the Kingdom of Mercia. The name Bakewell, meaning a spring or stream, and the Doomsday Book showed a settlement, a church and a mill. Nearby houses are Chatsworth House and Haddon Hall. A Motte and Bailey castle was built circa the 12th century. A market was established in 1254, which allowed Bakewell to thrive as a trading centre. The grade I listed five arched bridges over the River Wye (a magnet for painters and sightseers alike) dated from the 13th century. Also, the grade I listed is Holme Bridge, dated around 1664, which crosses on the northeastern outskirts of the town. A Chalybeate spring was discovered, and a bathhouse was built in 1697, which then led to an 18th-century attempt to develop Bakewell as a spa town. The building of Lumford Mill by Richard Arkwright in 1777 was followed by the rebuilding of much of the town in the 19th century. The mill, built in 1782 and employing over 300 people, housed its workers in cottages and was later sold to the Duke of Devonshire in 1860. Fire damaged in 1868, it was later rebuilt and is now a grade I listed building, well, some of it is. There are some 183 listed buildings in the town. Bakewell attracts visitors from all over, and Monday is the traditional market day.

Known for its Bakewell Tart and Bakewell pudding, a jam pastry with a filling enriched with egg and ground almonds, the Bakewell Tart is quite different and made with shortcrust pastry, an almond topping and a sponge and jam filling. The famous Mr Kipling also made the Cherry Bakewells, one of my favourite little treats. The origins of these tarts are not quite clear, but one story goes that the combination began by accident in 1820.

The landlady of the White Horse Inn, now the Rutland's Arms, left instructions for her cook to make a jam tart with an egg and almond paste pastry base. The cook, however, spread the almond paste on top of the jam instead of mixing them into the pastry. When cooked, the jam rose through the pastry, with the result being so successful it became a popular confection at the Inn. Commercial variations, usually with icing sugar on top, have spread the name.

There are three shops in Bakewell that all claim to be selling what they claim is the original recipe. The Bakewell Tart shop and coffee house sell four variations. The old original Bakewell Pudding shop and Bloomers of Bakewell both sell a Bakewell pudding of their own. I tried one of the many tarts made and sold by the Bakewell Tart shop, and enjoyable as it was, I am quite happy to buy and eat a common Mr Kipling cake from the local supermarket at less than half the price.

On a darker note, the town is also famous for the Stephen Downing murder conviction. Poor Stephen Downing was a 17-year-old lad who was a bit backward and found guilty of the murder of a legal secretary in Bakewell Cemetery in 1974. After a campaign by the local newspaper, which started an investigation, his conviction was overturned in 2002, by which time the poor bugger had spent 27 years in prison. Considered being the longest miscarriage of justice in British legal history. The very thought of it is beyond thinking. 27 years, what a waste of a person's life. Apparently, if memory serves, the police, seeing he was simple, helped him along with his statement and memory, as they do.

Bakewell is a delightful town to walk around. Sitting on a bench opposite the Rutland Arms with a bag of fish-n-chips while people watching, passed many an hour. Then going back to the bridge and sitting outside one of the little cafes with a cup of coffee and a Bakewell Tart past another enjoyable hour or so. After a relaxing night in the motorhome, watching all the tourists walking back across the bridge to their cars before heading home for a satisfying opportunity to recharge the batteries, I put my head down before doing the whole thing again the next day.

Sometimes I feel I should make an effort to get out there at night and visit one of the many pubs in or around the many towns and villages I visit throughout the country, but in all honesty, and without wishing to sound a miserable old bugger, I find myself becoming less and less interested. For one thing, and I think it's maybe the main reason, I find people are becoming, or seem to be, more miserable. I've gone into pubs both alone and with my lovely wife, Bet, before she left me, and my feeling has been the same. We've walked into pubs only to see people sitting there with faces as long as Livery Street (a long street in Birmingham). No conversation, no cheery banter. I've stood by the bar watching couples sitting and watching their drinks without talking to each other. I like to imagine during the daytime, it's totally different, where people are lively and excited. There is a distinct atmosphere from the day to the night. Unfortunately, I just don't enjoy drinking during the day.

Younger Bet and I would fly somewhere and be out every night in the hotel bars and local pubs. Slowly, over the years, we would see a different dynamic. People are just getting too miserable. Maybe it's the continuous recessions we have been having since the mid-70s. First, the debilitating strikes in the country, followed by the recessions of the mid-80s and then the mid-90s. How much more can we take, I ask you. No, I have to come to terms with it. When there is some entertainment on, and the weather is nice and warm, it's brilliant to sit outside and enjoy the music and ambience. Abroad, I'm still up for it, of course, but normally, around England, I don't go around gallivanting. I enjoy my own company, so it's quite satisfying to sit on my own, enjoying my own company and writing my books, of course.

Just a short seven-mile ride from Bakewell lies the village of Eyam, pronounced *eem*, famous for its plague, the black death in 1665/1666. Lead was mined in the area from Roman times, and many mines still run under the village to the present day. The parish Church of St Lawrence dates from the 14th century, but evidence of an earlier church can be found in the Saxon font. Owing to the newly discovered rich vein of lead during the 18th century, mining continued into the 19th century. In the 1841 census, some 960 people lived in the village, chiefly employed in agriculture, lead mining, cotton and silk weaving. By 1881, most men either worked in lead mining or in the manufacture of boots. Today, most of its income is tourist based.

The history of the plague began in 1665 when a flea-infested bundle of cloth arrived from London for Alexander

Hadfield, the local tailor. Within a week, his assistant George Vicars noticed the bundle was damp and opened it up to discover fleas. Before long, he was dead. More began dying in the household soon after. As the disease spread, they turned for leadership to their rector, who introduced several precautions to slow the spread. This included the arrangement that families were to bury their own dead. Church services were relocated, allowing villagers to separate themselves. Perhaps the best decision was that the entire village went under voluntary quarantine to prevent the further spread of the disease. Merchants from surrounding villages would leave supplies on marked rocks, and the villagers would leave the money in marked holes, which they would fill with vinegar to disinfect.

The plague ran its course over 14 months, with one account saying it killed at least 260 villagers out of a population of some 350. The church in Eyam has a record of 273 individuals who were victims of the plague. What is amazing is the survival amongst those within the community who were in close contact with those who died but never caught the disease. Elizabeth Hancock was unaffected, yet she buried six children and her husband in eight days. The graves are known as the Riley Graves, after the farm where they lived. (They still sit in a stone circle just outside the village). The unofficial gravedigger, Marshall Howe, also survived unaffected despite handling many infected bodies. Some villagers, amazingly, just had a natural resistance to the bubonic plague.

Plague Sunday has been celebrated in the village since the plague bicentenary in 1866, originally held in mid-august. It now takes place in Cucklett Delph, coinciding with the much older wake week and well-dressing ceremonies. An interesting titbit to this story is in the present day, there are still quite a few hundred people who live and can trace their family tree back to that plague. Joan Plant was born in her grandmother's house and can trace her history back to 1531. She met her husband at the local school. According to legend, her distant relative Margarete Blackwell contracted the plague in 1666. Whilst suffering a desperate thirst, she drank bacon fat, thinking it was milk. Immediately she vomited but made a speedy recovery. It seems survival is in Joan's genes. In the year 2000, an American biologist visited the village and conducted some research on 100 local people who could trace their roots back to the plague. He was looking for the delta 32 genes, a mutation that contains immunity to HIV. 14% of the people tested had the delta 32, a much higher than average percentage.

Another delightful destination I visited was Buxton. Just fifteen miles west of Bakewell. A spa town in high peak Derbyshire, it is England's highest market town on the edge of the Peak District National Park. Famous for its St Ann's Well, fed by a geothermal spring and bottled by the Buxton Mineral Water Company as well as Poole's cavern. Yet another beautiful town. There are many historic houses and buildings in Buxton, including John Carr restored Buxton Crescent. Buxton grew in importance in the late 18th century, with a resurgence a century later as the Victorians were drawn to the reputed healing powers of its waters. Initially a Roman settlement, many signs can be seen in its Roman names for its waters, Aquae Arnemetiae (baths of the grove goddess) and Batham gate (road to the bathhouse).

By 1460, Buxton Springs had been pronounced as a holy one dedicated to St Anne. The spring waters are piped to St Anne's Well, a shrine from medieval times where people can and do, bring containers and fill them up with water. Opposite the crescent and below the slope near the town centre, it was once called one of the seven wonders of the peak.

The Duke of Devonshire got involved when William Cavendish used profits from his copper mines to develop it as a spa town like Bath. Their ancestor, Bess of Hardwick, brought one of her four husbands, the Earl of Shrewsbury, to take the waters. Shortly after, he became the gaoler of Mary Queen of Scots. He took Mary there in 1573. He wanted her fit and well before chopping her head off on the block.

Along with Matlock, Buxton's profile was boosted by Erasmus Darwin, a friend of Josiah Wedgwood, whose family often visited Buxton. Two of Charles Darwin's half-cousins settled here. Buxton also, like many other villages, is steeped in its well-dressing festival that runs in July, running in its current form since 1840 to mark the provision of fresh water to the town's marketplace. As well as the dressing of the wells, it also includes a carnival procession and funfair (well dressing is an ancient custom unique to the peak district and dates back to Roman and Celtic times). Where communities would give thanks for the supply of fresh water.

Buxton had a base for British and Canadian troops in the First World War, with a hospital set up at the Buxton hydropathic hotel—after a decline in the early 20th century, it had a resurgence in the 1950 and 70s as a base for exploring the Peak District. At the south edge of the town, the River Wye has carved an extensive limestone cavern known as Poole's Cavern. Over 330 yards from its chambers are open to the public. Still known as a spa town, it has become increasingly popular with visitors coming from afar. The town centre is pedestrianised with a variety of shops selling everything from hardware to antiques, with plenty of seating in the form of concrete blocks from one end to the other. I tried the fish-n-chips at the Golden Fry smack bang in the centre, which was very nice but cut very thin. This is not like the fish I am used to having, which I would say is about three times as thick. A consolation is the parking bay just before entering the town from Chapel En Le Frith and next to the viaduct for coaches and buses, presumably motorhomes as well. At any rate, I spent a couple of nights on it along with two other motorhomes, though the traffic can get noisy.

Just five miles north of Buxton lies Chapel En Le Frith. Another beautiful little town is dubbed the Capital of the Peaks because of its proximity to the Peak District. The upper land areas became known as the Saxon lands, with the Viking lands coming as far as Sheffield. Established by the Normans in the 12th century, originally as a hunting lodge within the forest of High Peak, it was this that led to its name, Chapel in the Forest. Although most of the area is outside the national park itself, the town is in the western part of the Peak District. To the north and south lie the dark peak highlands. Heather-covered moorlands, rugged and bleak Chinley Churn and South Head are further on, with Kinder Scout looming above the entire area.

The Cromwellian era stocks for the punishment of petty crimes (i.e. nicking a loaf or an apple by the poor and starving) still stands on the side of Chapel En Le Frith marketplace, a square of cobbles adjacent to the stocks marks the spot where according to legend Will Scarlet, the legendary companion and step-brother to Robin Hood, is said to have died in 1283. Opposite the stocks is a pleasant little café where Bet and I sat and enjoyed a coffee and scone as we reflected on the history of the stocks. What did Will Scarlet die of? Was he murdered or just suffered, say, a heart attack? Maybe he suffered a heart attack after being released from the stocks?

HIDDEN WALKS
AROUND THE PEAKS

Three miles outside of Chapel En le Frith lies the Bugsworth basin, yet another place we had never heard of till seeing a reference to it on one of the various camping and motorhome sites. Basin? But there are hundreds of basins around the country, most of them attractive. But the Bugsworth Basin is special. For one, it has some beautiful walks along the canal and surrounding area. Another is its history.

Bugsworth Basin is the last complete example of a canal and tramway interchange in Britain, where limestone and gritstone were brought to the basin on the Peak Forest Tramway. Bugsworth Basin and Upper Peak Forest Canal were opened for trade in August 1796. Because of the demands of the industrial revolution, it soon became inadequate, so the Peak Forest Canal Company agreed in 1837 to construct the new Brook Course Branch Canal, which opened and was operational in 1841.

Nowadays, known as the lower basin, the villagers call it the 'New Drop'. Tramway wagons discharged their loads of stone down onto the wharf below, where it was hand loaded onto the barges by bargees into the boats, each carrying 25 tonnes. Pity those poor barge workers. On the left of the canal are the remains of the stone crusher house built by the railway company to produce ballast for railway construction, which superseded the canals as more economic. To the lower basin arm are the remains of a goods warehouse spanning the width of the arm. Built in 1860, no records survive for its purpose though it is known that bleached cloth from Forge Mill Bleach Works was transported to Bugsworth Basin by tramways, so its possible this was stored in the warehouse before being taken by canal to a mill near Marple for further processing. A reconstructed horse transfer bridge now spans the entrance to the lower basin arm. The arm and wharfage now include the foundations of the warehouse. A settled floor and evidence of a tramway can still be seen, along with a drainage valve and the base of a valve crane on the south side.

Gritstone slabs and slates for roofing were brought in from Cracken End quarries owned by a branch of the Carrington's at Ashen Cough. Much of this went to the growing towns of Manchester and Stockport, as did the pinkish freestone from Christ Quarry, which supplied the mullions and quoins to Bugsworth Hall. Coal was also delivered down to the wharf from Clough Pit, Dolly Pit, Lady Pit and Bugsworth Ball Pit. All newly opened for carrying by the tramways to distant, as to then, undreamed of markets. On land sold to the company, the Navigation Inn was built and also served as a shop supplying goods to the local community, as well as a shop. It also had a canal carrier's office and purpose-built stabling for the towing horses.

The Bugsworth family, who lived in the town and after whom the town was named in the early 1500s and was known as a respectable, thriving family who helped establish the community and was, interestingly, one of the very few families that a town was named after rather than the other way round where people were named after the place or town.

Arriving at the basin, I pulled down on the right-hand side next to the waste-emptying disposal point, toilets, and water tap. To the left is the canal basin, and to the right is a river.

I backed onto the river, giving me the sound of rushing water from the Weir. A very nice guy from Stoke-on-Trent named Chris, who was living on his barge nearby, opened the water tap for me, allowing me to fill my tank. My plan was to only spend one night before heading off somewhere else, but I felt so relaxed and comfortable that I ended up spending three nights. Besides, I wanted to have a little mooch in my Avon Dingy and 2-stroke engine along the canal. Beautiful as it is. I don't know if it is permissible to park alongside the canal. Certainly, I saw no signs saying otherwise. At any rate, the Navigation Pub allows stopovers if you have a meal or a drink.

Just 200 yards along the basin and at the head of the bridge, I called into the inn for a meal which I found adequate but pretty small in a portion. Why is portion control coming into everything? Going for the Cumberland sausage served on a bed of mash with peas, I wasn't overly impressed. The Cumberland sausage was just that, sausage, not a Cumberland as I know it, but rather a circle of half-inch thick sausage in a roll served on a soup plate. I had to have some biscuits when I got back to the van, as I was still hungry. Thankfully, someone directed me to the local Tesco, a quarter of a mile along the canal bank, where I bought some supplies. I would have happily gone to the Navigation again, but then I would have had to have a sweet to follow. Ahhh, yes, now we've got it, hence the smaller portions. Oh well.

Ford Hall, in the east of the town of Chapel, was the home of the Reverend William Bagshaw, the Apostle of the Peak, after he was ejected from the vicarage of Chinley. The village of Combes nearby gives its name to Combes' reservoir. In the rolling hills between the two lies Bank Hall, which is well worth a visit. Also, while we were in the area, we visited the beautiful village of Parwich, voted one of the most desirable places to live in the Sunday times. Being nosey, we wanted to have a look.

Due to its size, many places in the Peak District go undiscovered. From its hidden natural attractions like stunning waterfalls to its abundance of quaint little villages dotted around, Parwich is just one of them. A neat limestone village situated remotely in the scenic hill country of the white peak that is a little gem in the Derbyshire hillsides. An ideal base for touring the surrounding countryside, given the number of walking trails. Close by are the High Peak Trail and the Tissington Trail, both following the routes of former railway lines, so they are flat and level. The Limestone Way is a long-distance footpath that stretches for 46 miles between Castleton and Rocester and passes through the village.

With lanes lined with clusters of pretty stone cottages dotted along the stream that runs through the centre of the village, walking the quiet streets is like stepping back in time. The village is at the heart of some of the most beautiful country in Derbyshire, with the 18th-century mansion house nestling against Parwich Hill. Quiet as it is, the village only offers a little country pub, the Sycamore Inn, that also houses the village shop in a small room of the bar. Despite this, the village thrives, boasting a school, British Legion Club, and various sporting clubs. It's also shrouded in history, with several Roman coins being found in the place. Nearby are medieval buildings and remains of Roman field systems. We parked in Tissington next to the trail and walked into Parwich from there, a two-mile walk. There is a beautiful four-mile round walk that starts from Tissington and takes you into Parwich. The 411 bus service from Ashbourne stops in Parwich, but it only runs from 4-10 pm.

The Peak District doesn't have many hidden walks left. Britain's first national park is quite compact with homes and communities and visitors who enjoy romping uphill and down Dale, geddit? Down Dale. Many people live within an hour's drive of the region, us included.

1. Coomb Dale.
   Start/finish at Eyam free car park. The Peak District dark peak distance 9 miles from Coomb Dale is pretty quiet, maybe because of its lack of panoramic views.

2. Margery Hill and outer edge.
   Start/finish at Langsett Reservoir car park, the peak district, dark peak distance 10.6 miles. Six miles outer edge and Margery Hill are just a few miles up from Langsett Reservoir and offer big skies and nice rolling hills with one or two other walkers enjoying the trail.

3. Lantern Pike.
   Start/finish Sett Valley trail car park with a distance of some 9.2 miles. The 61 high peak bus from Buxton to Glossop stops at the car park. Whilst a quiet walk, the bonus here is the friendly pub with the same name at the bottom, the Lantern Pike Inn.

4. Axe Edge Moor.
   Start/finish at the layby parking on the A54, a distance of 10 miles. Offering quieter walking above the moorland. It sticks to the Whetstone Ridge and Axe Edge Moor. From there, you can see the unique peaks of Chrome and Parkhour Hills -the dragon's back in the near distance.

5. Ramshaw Rock.
   The start/finish is the layby parking on Roaches Road. The Peak District, White Peak, distance 7 miles. Ramshaw Rock offers a great alternative to watch the sunrise away from the crowds, good clambering above black brook nature reserve with views over to Mermaids Pool and Merryton Low. If you start early enough, you can miss the crowds that get on the Roaches.

6. Gun.
Start/finish roadside parking in Danebridge distance of
7.7 miles. This is a small but well-formed hill with great
views. It's not as popular as other walks and is relatively
unknown. If you start from Danebridge, the route crosses
pretty weirs and natural pools, plus a great little boozer
called The Ship just up the hill into Wincle.

7. Wild Bank.
Start/finish at Stalybridge Train Station with a distance of
some 8.4 miles. This great little hill offers a quiet spot to
watch the sunset over Manchester. Whilst the moors are
peppered with reservoirs, you will hike high enough to
feel above them all.

8. Chew Valley and Wimberry Crags.
Start/finish at the Dovestone Reservoir car park, a distance
of some 6.9 miles. The Dovestone Circular boasts Birches
Clough and the Trinnacle, a very popular walk in the Peak
District. While Chew offers a windswept aspect, it's the
ramble along Wimberry Crags and down to Alphin Pike
that gives the most stunning views across Manchester and
over the valley down to Dovestone.

9. South Head and Chinley Churn.
Start/finish Chinley Train Station distance 8.5 miles. Just over
the valley from Edale are the towns of Chinley and Chapel En
Le Frith. From the former, you can wander up to Cracken
Edge and Chinley Churn to sit on the rock overlooking
Chinley from Cracken Edge. The views are stunning. Mostly
used by local walkers, it makes a great walk.

A great list of walks app can be downloaded onto your
phone called VISORANDO. It's free and will give you every
walk in the country. Indeed, you will be saturated with walks
to your heart's content. Go find it, download it and enjoy.

THE YORKSHIRE DALES

From the centre of the Derby Dales to roughly the centre of the Yorkshire Dales, it is less than 90 miles. From my home in Sutton Coldfield, it's only circa 130 miles. Each is equally stunning and beautiful as the other. I have always been torn between the two. Still am. In fact, if you factor in Wales, also about 100 miles to the coast, it makes a bit of a tough choice which one to go for on any break. Ooohhhh, life is so hard.

I love that statement coming from the guy I met in Spain, parked up in the free car park next to a very nice beach with shops and restaurants within a short walk. When he sets off from England, he waits till he gets to Calais before deciding whether to go right or left. What a beautiful concept. It encapsulates everything about the motorhome. The utter freedom, the idea that you can just get up and go wherever you want when you want.

With a tent, you have that freedom, of course, if you like lying on wet, lumpy ground. Well, I'm not knocking that, and I know from my grandkids that things have improved nowadays. They sleep on raised beds and have all the comforts. Oh no, I just couldn't put up with all that hassle, putting up the tent, taking down the tent. Taking it out to dry it before repacking, making sure you have all the pegs, poles and cooker parts together before packing away. Oh lord, no, I'm in pain now just thinking about it. Tenting is for the young, the teenagers, and the kids. I passed that stage many moons ago.

The caravan gives you a certain freedom of course, ok, where shall we go next month? The Derby Dales are only some 40-50 miles away, but where do we stop? We must find a campsite before we set off. That's the first problem, then the second is the packing and the unpacking, the chairs, the tables, the garden furniture. That's before and after you have all that towing to and fro to get wherever you're going. Swinging side to side on the motorways to driving down narrow lanes by the skin of your teeth. Oh, no, no, no.

When I get into my little motorhome, my baby, I simply decide which way I'm heading, left or right? Just like that guy I met in Spain. North, South, East or West. Very rarely East in England, I'm afraid. East is not too much fun.

My little camper is packed with everything I can think of that I'm going to need or use as I travel around Europe, either for a few days or a few months. I don't watch my weight like a girl watches her diet. My Autotrail Cheyenne 2.8 turbo averages out at 20 miles per gallon, whether uphill or down dale, motorway running or normal road use. I don't overload it, but considering it's a six berth and working out the average weight of a human at, say, ten stone, then it's certainly not overweight.

My bed is made up and cleaned, ready for use with a lightweight quilt, my trusty little clock ticking away. My wardrobe is full of all the clothes I think I'm going to wear for walking around the port or beach (shorts usually) for the beach swimming shorts, at least three pairs. A jacket and smart slacks for those nights out. Well, you never know. Plus, heavy weather coats according to and as needed around England. In and out, in and out. My overhead cab bed has its own bedding, folded and ready to make up if ever the grandkids decide to give me the pleasure of their company wherever I am in the world.

Typically Sammy, my granddaughter, will text me, "Grandad, I've got a ten-day break coming up." One year I was in Igoumenitsa in northern Greece when she texted. The nearest airport was on the island of Corfu opposite. Checking with the nearest ferry company, it quoted me £160 for a one-way ticket to Venice from Igoumenitsa. A great saving on travelling through Albania, Montenegro, Bosnia and Serbia. Texting her, we arranged to pick her up from Marco Polo Airport three days later. That gave me time for the overnight trip plus two days to find a campsite before picking her up from the airport. After paying £65 for a return ticket, she had a lovely cheap break and a tour of the canals around Venice. With the extra few quid I gave her, I think she had a lovely time. Things like that happen regularly, whether in England or abroad.

My overhead cupboards are stacked with all kinds of foods that will last for months if not a couple of years, packet and tinned soups, sealed coffees, chocolates and tea, Fray Bentos pies, always handy when nothing else is available, costing a pound, and together with a small 40 pence tin of beans or peas I have a ready meal within twenty minutes. My other cupboards are packed with shoes, maps, a sewing kit and bandages. Never forget the bandages, plasters, dressings and cream. Most times, I never use them, but you never know. I carry every major international plug I can think of, having once got stuck in Morocco and in big trouble except for the kindly help of a friendly French group of fellow campers. It taught me a lesson when I realised I didn't have the right adaptor. Then there is my inverter, for converting my twelve volts to 240 volts when I'm wild camping, most times abroad, and in fact, around England. Not forgetting my rooftop solar panels, 100 watts which is quite adequate for my lights, television and computer. My only regret is that I never had 200 watts. No, maybe 300 watts even.

The Yorkshire Dales or the Derby Dales, the choice is yours, and it can be a bit difficult to decide. The Peak District is smaller and closer to Manchester and Sheffield and is popular with those looking for a day out. It has very nice market towns and is divided into two areas by geology. The Dark Peaks to the north are gritstone with moorland tops. Think kinder. The White Peaks to the south are limestone that is more fertile and grass-covered. The dales cover a much larger area and have much more diverse scenery. The valleys are larger and wider, but again, there are several attractive towns to use as a base or to visit. For walking, maybe the peak district has the edge with plenty of rail trails on closed railway lines, ideal for cyclists and walkers. For stately homes, the Peak District has places like Chatsworth and Haddon Hall, but both have ruined castles. Both have caves open to the public.

The Yorkshire Dales National Park was established in 1954 and is an upland area of the Pennines in the historic county of Yorkshire, rising from the Vale of York westwards to the hilltops of the Pennine watershed in Ribblesdale Dentdale and Garsdale. It extends westwards across the watershed, but most of the valleys drain eastwards to the Vale of York into the Rivers Ouse and the Humber. The extensive limestone cave systems are a major area for caving in the United Kingdom. And many walking trails run through the hills and dales.

The Yorkshire Dales are surrounded by the north Pennine and Orton Fells in the north, the Vales of York and Mowbray to the east. The south Pennines in the south and the Lake District to the west spread to the north from the market towns of Settle Skipton and Harrogate in the north to Wharfedale and Airedale.

Makes your choice and take your pick.

BURNSALL is a quiet, charming little village which has the River Wharf running through it. The stone bridge was

MEANDERING AROUND ENGLAND IN A MOTORHOME

charming just to sit at and have a picnic. We also camped up there and spent the night. The village is overlooked by Burnsall Fell, which holds the oldest fell race in England. 1000s turn up to participate.

MUKER is set on the hillside above the River Swale and is home to the highest inn in England, THE TAN HILL INN. Very popular with motor homers and locals alike. The food is excellent, the atmosphere is great, and it holds regular music events. It is always popping up on camping and motorhome forums, and we've spoken to people who actually travel miles to visit the place just to say they have stayed there. The village dates back hundreds of years and has lots of history, yet it has hardly changed. Popular with walkers, it has plenty of bed n breakfasts, two pubs and a craft store.

GRASSINGTON. One of the largest villages in the Yorkshire Dales, again beautiful with its cobbled streets, it's the perfect place for walks as it's the start of several circular routes.

KETTLEWELL. Featured in the film The Calendar Girls, Kettlewell is a charming village, friendly and relaxed. The film captures it well. Home to pretty stone and brick-built 17th and 18th-century cottages. It has three pubs and a shop, two cafes and a petrol station, a small one.

PATELEY BRIDGE is home to the oldest sweetshop in the world and is a great village to use as a base for exploring the dales. Apparently, Pateley Bridge has been an inspiration for writers and artists for generations. When you walk around it, you can see why.

MALHAM is a village I have visited twice, and each time, like Kettlewell, I've been impressed and in awe of its charm. Having a picnic at the top of Malham Cove was a delight, with its white-painted houses which line the tight, winding roads. It makes the perfect picture postcard of the Dales.

BUCKDEN, on the east bank of the River Wharfe, Buckden, is another charming small village not to be missed. With its small stone bridge, it makes for a beautiful place to spend a few hours. Very popular with walkers who come to take on the dales way, an 85-mile hike between Ilkley to Bowness in Windermere.

WEST BURTON, one of the larger villages in the dales, Burton has a local store café and bed n breakfast. 300m from the centre of the village is Cauldron Falls, a stunning, picturesque waterfall on the Walden Beck.

APPLETREEWICK, with its picturesque houses that date back to the 12th century and line the streets, and the New Inn pub is a popular resting place to explore the local area. Once a flourishing village in the 14th century, thanks to farming, it hasn't grown much, with less than 200 people living there.

LONG PRESTON on the edge of the Yorkshire Dales, a few miles from Skipton, the Boar's Head is popular with locals and tourists alike, but visit the village on a May Day, you will find the locals Maypole dancing on the village green. A tradition that goes back decades.

LEYBURN is worth a stop just to admire the views of the surrounding countryside

MASHAM is a must-see market town famous for its breweries, steam engines, and its annual sheep fair. Located on the banks of the River Ure. it is open to idyllic river walks and trails leading to historic follies and waterfalls.

MIDDLEHAM is home to the largest castle keep in the north of England, once home to Richard III. A traditional charming market town, it's a must-see thanks to its cobbled market square and Georgian tea rooms, which are delightful.

SKIPTON is known as the gateway to the dales and overlooks the Aire Gap, rich in natural beauty. It has the beautiful 900-year-old Skipton Castle.

HAWES, famous for its production of Wensleydale cheese, is blessed with mellow stone buildings, shops and houses linked by cobbled streets. The name Hawes means 'pass between mountains', obviously due to its position between the hills of Buttertubs and Fleet Moss.

RICHMOND is another rich Yorkshire town we visited and has hardly changed throughout the centuries. Richmond is a vibrant market town with plenty to keep you occupied with ghost walks and its castle keep. Even the oldest Georgian playhouse in the country.

REETH, if you must miss out on any village, don't miss out on visiting Reeth. Once a major site for lead mining, you will notice abandoned, ruined mine workings such as the old gang smelting mill built in 1790 and last used in 1899. A most fascinating place to visit.

Nice as the villages are in and around the Yorkshire Dales, I don't think they have the edge on the Peak District or the Derby Dales for diversity, interest or beautiful villages even the Dales, to me, have an intimacy that the Yorkshire Dales don't have.

What the Yorkshire Dales do have are the reservoirs, lots of them, many with pleasant walks around them. The Dales have miles upon miles of hiking and walking trails. Here are just a few that we have walked around, but there are at least 120 reservoirs. Spoil yourself, tuck in and fill your little pot, and wear your little legs out exploring and discovering.

GRIMWITH RESERVOIR, a hidden gem tucked away off the road between Grassington and Pateley Bridge. The first reservoir was built at Grimwith around 1856 by the Bradford Corporation. At the time, Bradford was desperate for more water for mill owners further down the River Wharfe, particularly in Otley. In the 60s, the reservoir was expanded and increased, raising by 20 meters. It provides a vital stop-off point for migrating waders, geese and ducks and a year-round population of birds. There is a beautiful four-mile walk around the lake, including the nature reserve set aside, all on a suitable surface. There is a free car park on site where we camped up for the night before our walk.

SCAR HOUSE and ANGRAM reservoir, this is a lovely seven-mile walk with stunning scenery, including the beautiful dam at Scar House. The loop trail is not too far from Harrogate, so it is perfect for a peaceful walk starting at Scar House car park.

FEWSTON RESERVOIR is on the edge of the Yorkshire dales, a not-too-arduous walk of some four miles, great for any level of walker walking along the side of the water or through the woods, offering superb views of the rolling hills of the dales.

EMBSAY RESERVOIR is a small reservoir that packs a punch. Starting from the free car park and only a mile long, you can head up to the summit of EMBSAY CRAG and enjoy stunning views just outside Skipton (the gateway to the dales).

LEIGHTON AND ROUNDHILL RESERVOIR. The ideal starting point here is the beautiful bridge over the reservoir. Follow the woodland path before climbing into the surrounding moors and enjoying stunning views back down over the beautiful waters at Nidderdale. You have great views of the countryside before heading down to nearby Masham, where you can enjoy a break and a pint.

BLACKMOOR FOOT RESERVOIR, a haven for wildlife, sits between Meltham and Slaithwaite. A short but pleasant walk through tranquil woodland with lovely views around it.

DIGLEY RESERVOIR. Digley Reservoir sits just below the small Bilberry reservoir, so you can walk the two if you feel up to it. We didn't. Just three miles from Holmfirth, so you can pop in for a pint or a snack after your walk.

YATEHOLME RESERVOIR is the highest of four reservoirs that sit above Holmbridge, a small reservoir giving fine views over the surrounding moors. If you feel fit enough and start early enough, you can also walk around nearby RAMSDEN RESERVOIR AND RIDINGS WOOD RESERVOIR.

MALHAM TARN is the highest lime-rich lake in the Dales, home to rare plants and animals, varied bird life and stunning views. Another walk from here is the Pennine Way from MALHAM VILLAGE, past Malham Cove and up into fountains fell. From Malham, there is another walk to the dramatic waterfall of Janet's Foss through ancient woodland covered in wild garlic and bluebells in spring, ending at the falls.

There are some 120-plus reservoirs and lakes in Yorkshire. Many of them allow for recreational use, like fishing or sailing. Quite a few, and I never made a point of counting, allow free parking. The busiest lakes and reservoirs have height barriers and parking charges, so you motor homers, like me, do your homework first. If you're heading for the busiest car parks near the busiest towns, you won't get into the car parks, or you will pay to get into them.

My preference is to find a quiet reservoir with a nice quiet out of the way and a free car park where I can spend the night, enjoy the tranquillity and peacefulness, and enjoy the ambience after a pleasant walk around the lake. Bliss! When I leave, I leave no rubbish, only my footprints. If it's dry, not even them.

THE LAKES

The lakes when you think of the lakes, you think of Coniston Water, Donald Campbell's Watery Grave, or Lake Windermere. My first experience of the Lake District was in the small town of Kendal, some 21 miles from Lake Coniston.

A lady had rung me up, asking for a price to move her from the town of Kendal to a small village in Cornwall. It was one of those experiences that made you open the window to how other people live their lives. I was running a transport company at the time in the mid-nineties; she had asked for a price which I gave her, allowing me to spread it over two days and with two men to do the job. Me and a friend, Micky Kirby.

Arriving at Kendal, we were greeted by a bit of a formidable-looking woman and shown what needed moving. All the furniture, old and battered, was spread across two floors in a bit of a grubby looking flat above a shop right in the centre. Over the two-day period, we got to know the story behind the actions of the lady and her family. Now most of us book a week or a fortnight's holiday in a place we like, whether it be in Sunny Spain, the Maldives or Portugal or even in the Lake District. This lady, together with her family or friends, had rented a flat over a two-year period. Instead of a holiday let price, they had got it at a much cheaper cost spread over a longer period. By spreading the cost out between the group, it whittled down to just a few hundred pounds spread between them. This enabled them to use the property as often or as little as they wanted, either as a group or individually, to enjoy the area as a base. At the end of the period, they would move on to somewhere else, i.e. Cornwall, where they enjoyed another long period. Brilliant, what a great idea. Some people buy a static caravan. In our case, we bought the motorhome; I know people who have rented the static out to cover the cost of the site fees. We are all different. We all find different ways to utilise our time and space, and money, of course.

This lady and her family, or group, had found a great way to live and get to know an area intimately over a period of a year or two, maybe longer. Whilst it wouldn't suit me, I could certainly see the sense of sharing. I know it's not unique. I've known of people who club together in a holiday apartment or villa. Some people are in a static caravan. If you think of the logic of it, a static caravan can be picked up for a mere few thousand pounds. Big money for the site owner only, of course, is in the site rental of, say, £3,000 per year and more. If a family or group of four spreads this between them, it breaks down to a more manageable £250 per group for three months of the year. Quite cheap, really, for a holiday break.

When I heard the English accent coming from a nice fancy yacht on the French Riviera, I couldn't help but stop and say hello. It turned out the guy owned a property nearby with his family and lived in the town. Somehow he had gotten into a group who had clubbed together and bought a quarter share in the yacht for an obviously reduced price. It was managed well, he told me, with no problems sharing the facilities, costings and everything pertaining to the yacht. If you think of the number of yachts that lie or sit empty, like holiday lets, month after month, you have to think. What a brilliant idea. I know. I had a yacht on the Devon coast. This very nice friendly guy was obviously a retired or semi-retired professional businessman. By buying a share in this yacht, he and his family gained all the benefits of living a quality few weeks on the sea without the crippling costs normally associated with such a lifestyle.

Kendal is a beautiful little town set in its own little time warp. With its quaint buildings, shops and cafes running off its cobbled streets, it makes a nice place to visit on its own merits. Kendal is a market town mainly with grey limestone buildings earning it the nickname "auld grey town," but don't be put off by that. It has a beauty all of its own. With the beautiful River Kent running through the centre, it makes for a nice backdrop with its stunning grey bridge. A market town, it is noted for its shops, festivals and historic sites, including Kendal Castle. And it's the famous Kendal Cake. In the south of the Lake District and six miles from the M6 motorway, it is also only a few miles from the sea, so makes it an ideal base to cater to everyone's holiday needs. With two castles, two museums, historical buildings and bridges, fine restaurants, quality hotels and pubs, there is also plenty to do. Some nine miles from Lake Windermere and 30 miles from Keswick, the other lakes are all within a short drive and are locations for pleasant walks and rambles.

Once the largest town in the county, it was once one of the chief manufacturing towns from the 14th century, with many mills on the River Kent, from which the town gained its name. With four bridges, it has plenty of ways in. Traditionally, its chief trade was wool. The town's motto, *"pannus mihi panis,"* means 'The wool is my bread'. (Well, there is plenty of grazing land around). The manufacturing died off after the canal was filled in and turned into building land footpaths and cycle paths. Historically, Kendal could have been on a par with York if it were not for its zealous council to move with the times. Home to a multitude of historic buildings from the 14th-century Castle Dairy, Kendal Castle and Castle Howe, a host of houses and museums dated from the 1600s to today. The Romans left them with the camp at Watercrook on the banks of the River Kent.

The Normans left behind two castles and a church that is only a few feet narrower than the York Minster. The Elizabethans and Victorians created and left a wealth of architecture that all goes to make Kendal a gem of a place to visit.

Lake Windermere is apparently the largest lake in England, never mind the largest lake within the Lake District National Park. In the north of the lake, trails lead off to Orrest Head with views across the lake and fells beyond, some ten miles long by one mile wide and 220 feet deep. It is home to Atlantic salmon and brown trout. The great north annual swim is held here, as well as other events, including sailing and swimming.

Coniston Water is the fifth largest lake amongst the lakes at about five miles long and half a mile wide, with the old man of Coniston towering over the lake and village. Half a mile down from the village of Coniston, you can hire boats and bikes to explore the area. With various jetties around the lake, there are sailings all year round. You can even steam along the lake on the Victorian steam Yacht gondola run by the national trust.

Lake Coniston is obviously most famous for its world speed-breaking records by Donald Campbell, who broke eight absolute world speed records in the 1950s and 60s and ended his life at the bottom of the lake, some 130-184 feet below. His attempt took place in January 1967, in which he attempted to better 300 mph, which he did. But his boat 'Bluebird,' shot up into the air and disappeared into the lake. It remained there with Donald's body until it was found in 2001. Once used as a fish source by the monks of Furness Abbey in the 13th and 14th centuries, it was later used to transport slate and ore from the many mines worked in the Coppermine; it has three small islands, each owned by the national trust. Victorian philosopher John Ruskin bought the Brantwood House in 1871 and declared its view over the lake to the Old Man of Coniston to be the best in England. Arthur Ransome based his book 'Swallows and Amazons' on Coniston Water, with locations dotted around the lake.

Places to visit around Coniston are HAWKESHEAD, the pretty village with its cobbled streets, pubs, shops and cafes, and the Beatrix Potter Gallery.

ESTHWAITE WATER, the small privately owned lake, was just two miles long, but with a pleasant walk along the footpath to the lake.

CONISTON COPPER MINES, you can download a self-guided trail here to see the remains of the copper mines with insights into how the copper mining industry developed and how the miners lived and earned their livings.

There are miles of walking routes around and without stiles, including TARN HOWS, HIGH YEWDALE AND YEWDALE BRIDLEWAY, MONK CONISTON AND CONISTON TO TORVER JETTY, all miles without stiles. There are even more walks around most of the lakes, some small and manageable rambles, others arduous. The largest national park is a gem of a place to visit. Breathtaking lakes and soaring mountains are known as fells, and each lake and valley has its own distinct character. Grasmere and Ryedale are two of the more peaceful and smaller lakes to visit with steady, pleasant walks. Grasmere village is full of charm, places to eat, and not forgetting its famous gingerbread cake.

ULLSWATER AND GLENRIDDING have stunning scenery with a good starting point for walkers and climbers alike. The Langdale Valley is also a great place for walks.

BUTTERMERE, CRUMMOCK AND LOWESWATER, known as the northern lakes, is probably the most peaceful part of the Lake District with many features of historical interest.

TARN HOWS, situated between the south lakes villages of Coniston and Hawkshead, gives stunning views of the fells and has a circular route ideal for a short walk, or it can be extended, taking you up to Black Crag.

ORREST HEAD. A must-see viewpoint, a short walk to the summit from Windermere gives amazing views.

LATRIGG, not so high, gives splendid views overlooking Keswick town. It even has a nice little bench overlooking the lake and town where you can sit, rest and contemplate.

LANTYS TURN, in the Ullswater Valley and just a short walk from Glenridding. You will spot red squirrels here or look for the ice house where ice was collected. A short walk will give magnificent views over the lake.

GUMMERS HOW. Off the beaten track, it's an ideal family walk with plenty of picnic spots and plenty of views over Windermere, Morecambe Bay and the central fells.

There are waterfalls, plenty to see and climb, like AIRA FORCE. No ordinary waterfall. This is a sheer display of power and beauty. It has to be seen to be believed with a climb to the top.

HARDKNOTT FORT This is the remains of a Roman fort built under Adrian's rule in the second century. Built as the headquarters for its commanding officer, it even has a bathhouse, free to visit. This is not for the motor homer, though. Hardknott Pass is one of the most difficult roads in the country and isn't for the fainthearted. We were offered a lift in an open-topped land rover by a local who kindly took us up.

HONISTER PASS, one of the most scenic and breathtaking routes in the Lake District, up from the eastern end of Borrowdale, drops into Buttermere with a gradient of 1 in 4.

203

The Ruskin Museum has a display of Donald Campbell memorabilia and is home to the tail fin of K7 and the air intake of the Bristol Orpheus engine, which was recovered in 2001. The aim is to return Bluebird to Coniston water before returning her to the Ruskin museum, perhaps a fitting end for it.

You don't go to the Lake District for the bright lights. Well, being one of the darkest areas in the country, it's also about the best place in England to look at the brightest stars in the night sky, but you get my drift. If you want to party, you go to Blackpool or Torquay, not the Lake District. You go to the Lake District for its beauty, its tranquillity, its stunning scenery, and its lakes.

The Lake District is England's largest national park and is now a world heritage site. Home to Scafell Pike its highest mountain, the country's highest mountain. Wastewater, its deepest lake surrounded by mountains, Red Pike, Kirk Fell great gable and Scafell Pike. Thriving communities like Kendal, Bowness on Windermere, and Keswick are dotted around and nestled in. The Lake District National Park Authority, with other organisations, protects and helps nurture the Lake District itself.

These are just a few of the many lakes, walks and places of interest around the Lake District. We visited over three separate periods over a couple of years. Each place we visit has its own beauty in its own particular way in its own time and season. The lakes are equally stunning in early spring or autumn, yet most people visit in the peak season of summer. Great in the one respect if you're in a car and maybe stopping in a hotel or guest house. In a fairly large motorhome, we prefer it when it's quieter.

It's difficult to choose between one of the many places we visit and continue to visit. The Derby Dales offer so much variety with its walks, Dales and towns like Bakewell, Buxton Ashbourne and Matlock Bath. In contrast, the Yorkshire Dales are stunning, with great walks, hikes and climbs. Different again is the new forest, Exmoor and Dartmoor, each again different with so much to offer, so much contrast. The New Forest ponies in one, the Exmoor ponies in another. As a contrast, again, I visit and enjoy the coastal resorts like Barmouth in Wales, St Ives, Falmouth in Cornwall, Torquay, and Weymouth in Devon. I would visit the English resorts far more if I was made welcome, but simply the main resorts don't want motor homers, even in low season. Much as I spend, and I do spend, your average holiday resort assumes we don't.

Bluntly they want people in for the day, the week or a fortnight, top whack and spending all their money. When a tourist goes home skint, the holiday resorts love it. We campers spend our money over a longer period, over the year, but we have to buy our stock from somewhere, drinks, food. Even from the supermarket we are spending and buying, as mentioned earlier in Barmouth, the car parks along the seafront stretch for almost a mile. For the biggest part of the year, they are empty. Even at the height of the season, they only fully fill up on the bank holidays.

I wrote and suggested to the council that for the sake of one or two thousand pounds, they could put a water supply tap and tipping facilities in and charge 5-8- or 10 per night to park up for the night. First, you have the income from parking, then if we spent £20 at the local Co-op, it is better than nothing. A pint or two in one of the boozers, maybe a couple of portions of fish-n-chips. It's all useful income for a town that doesn't have a lot coming in. At one stage, Barmouth, like many resorts, was almost dying on its feet. Half a brain makes you think they might capitalise on it. Holidaymakers, as a rule, come away during the eight-week main period of July and August. Motor homeowners go away all year round.

The last time I took my grandkids, I spent circa £300 over three days. I used to go quite a bit in the winter, but their attitude continues to put me off. I haven't been to Weston-Super-Mare for years. I am very selective about where I go because of their attitude. I find myself more and more preferring to go abroad. In France, the attitude is totally and utterly different. Why I don't know, but Aires abound throughout France and Europe. Without the Aires, there are far more places to park. Though, with the increasing number of motorhomes, that might not be the case in the future. There again, it might even improve if the councils see the benefits or potential benefits.

EPILOGUE

We are all but a mere nit on a gnat's testicle, a grain of sand in the desert, a fleck of dust in the universe. We all come into the world with no hair and no teeth, wrinkled up by little bunches of skin. We go out of the world the same. But it's the in-between. We are all supposed to be born equal under god. What an utter load of nonsense.

Prince Charles has just inherited almost a billion pounds upon becoming King after the passing of his mother, the Queen. Long live the King; this is what we are told about. In turn, the King passed over the Duchy of Cornwall to his son William who became next in line to the throne, worth one and a half billion and an income for life and beyond, tax-free. That's what we are told about. Lucky little Prince William and his lovely wife Kate, even luckier their children, especially firstborn Prince George. Not so lucky for the rest of them. Look at Prince Harry, the spare, poor bugger filled with resentment and jealousy.

This is without all the swans they own, even the shoreline around our country. How can it be right that one family can own the shoreline around the country, along with all the minerals that go with it? Then there are the houses, the palaces, the castles, the houses within the castles, the houses within the palaces, plenty enough to go around for a few generations, and aren't they lucky? Those, even on the periphery, get a little house, well, a little house to them, a mansion to us mere peasants. And with the little house goes a few million quid inheritance and the guarantee of a nice job in the city. Along with a nice job in the city goes the guarantee of a nice happy marriage to a multi-millionaire at least, and hard as their lives are, much as they plead and cry for privacy, don't they just love it when those cameras pop at the wedding and red carpet attendances.

Ok, it's all imploding at the moment with Prince Harry marrying his actress or ex-actress wife, Meghan, who is leading him by the nose like a little lamb towards superstardom and billionaire status. Nasty and narcissistic as she is, she knows a good touch when she sees one, and the royal family is a good touch. Harry, in particular, is a lovely little touch. It's only when you see them step out of that little bubble you see how vulnerable they are, how human they are.

Don't get me wrong, I'm not anti-monarchy. What is the alternative? Donald Trump? I'm not jealous, and I'm certainly not bitter, but we left the medieval period behind a long time ago. I well remember the Queen visiting Birmingham in the mid-50s, and thousands lined the streets with flags and our little presentation mugs, waving like lunatics. But where did those flags come from? Who paid for them? Not my mom or dad. It was accepted and spoken about that various government councils covered up ugly buildings and areas that Queen Victoria and Queen Elizabeth passed by. Not for them the ugly truth and bluntness of our surroundings.

Who remembers the furore when the Royal Family asked for more money towards the cost of the upkeep of the palaces, guards, processions, etc.? Well, not exactly the Royal Family themselves. It's the minions hanging onto the ermine who do the asking, the demanding. In turn, they get titles, knighthoods or OBEs. The costings were up to some million quid a year, maybe more, and when they were questioned about how much the royal family were worth, they came back screaming that far from being billionaires were only worth some 300 million. Far less than Paul McCartney, worth circa 800 million at the time. Well, he soon dropped that figure as well when his divorce started, and he realised how much he could lose.

It was pointed out quickly that many, if not all, the palaces and castles were not, in fact, owned by the royal family but by us, the public, you and me. That is so funny. It's, of course, why we (the taxpayers) are spending billions on repairs and renovations to Buckingham Palace. But it's telling that at one Buckingham Palace garden party (well, they have to have them), someone had the temerity to ask the Queen how she felt about all these 1000s of people trampling about on the palace lawns? Tellingly, and with a glint in her eye, she replied, "Well, how would you feel about total strangers trampling all over your lawn?" Hmmmm. There we go, then. We are total strangers trampling about on lawns that we own.

Four hundred years ago and longer, we stood for this. Even as little as 200, 150 years ago, we had to bow our heads and touch our forelocks to our superiors, the coal mine owners, mill owners and factory owners, all in line and order of importance down from the royal family. You only have to read some of Catherine Cookson's books to give you a taste of the times. Who remembers the kings and queens of old being anointed by God to rule over us? Not voted in by majority vote mind, anointed. And we believed it. Who believed they actually had blue blood? I did. I even believed they never went to the toilet like us mere mortals. How thick is that? The fact is, we have been conned for over 2000 years. Before that, we were just whipped into submission. After that, we were brainwashed into doing as we were told, or we would go to hell in a handcart.

The choice is simple: follow God's rules as laid down in stone, the ten commandments, instructed to find and be brought down from the mountain by Moses and live in paradise. Or don't follow them and spend the rest of eternity burning in hell. Few people wanted the latter, me included. With certain races, it varied slightly. One race was guaranteed 36 vestal virgins if they toed the line, or was it 36,000. It doesn't matter; we had to toe the line while those at the top were chopping our heads off at will, at God's will, while sending us out, robbing countries around the world and making themselves richer all the time. How great is that?

I grew up in the backstreets and so-called slums of Birmingham, Summer Lane, Aston and Rocky Lane, and Nechells, with outside toilets and the daily mail to wipe our a**es. A Belfast sink and cold water. If we wanted a bath, we had to boil saucepans on the four-ring gas cooker. If you couldn't afford the saucepans or the gas, you went without and stunk unless you got to the weekly swimming baths, free with the school group.

I accepted all this growing up as part of life; I know most of my peers and my neighbours did. We were p**s poor because we had no money; we were poor because we were uneducated and stupid. It was our fault. We were told this regularly by our teachers, our betters, but as I got older, I questioned my position. As I looked around, I saw people who were determined to climb out of the slum hole they were buried up to their necks in, the shopkeeper, the coalman, the tatter, or the scrap man. Only one or two made it. Others turned to villainy or thieving. If you've got no brains or prospects, an easy way out. Well, even if you're sharp and got brains, there is an easy way out.

I was lucky; I had my wife behind me and eventually started my transport business. At any time, things could have fallen apart. I could have given up at the first hurdle. Our marriage could have failed within years, setting me back to zero starts.

I saw it happen many times. When you lose your hard-earned money at forty, it's hard to get back on the bandwagon. At fifty, it's harder. At sixty, you can forget it. Trust me, I know it. I've seen it many times. Along with our personal fortunes, society changed after World War II. Which followed and directly resulted from World War I, each a war not of our making. Things got better. Slums were being cleared, and better housing was made available. Prospects were looking brighter and more optimistic for far more people.

None of us was ever told this back in the day, though. No one ever turned around to my classmates or me and said, "Have hope, children. We're all going through a hard time, but things will pick up and get better." I well remember that one day when one girl of 14 had the temerity to ask, "What do you think we will do when we leave school, sir?"

With a sneering sniff as he looked down his pince nez glass and gave us our future in just a few short sentences. "Well, the girls will no doubt get a job at Woolworths until they are 17, then get married. The boys will get work as labourers or factory workers. Those who are lucky and work hard might get an apprenticeship. Some of you will no doubt end up in prison."

Looking around the class of some 30ish, who looked as equally stunned as I was feeling, I thought that was our future tied up in a nice little bundle. It also opened up my eyes and mind to how the teachers themselves looked at us as human beings. By hook or by crook, I was determined that my life was going to be different.

After we got married, I took the enormous step of buying the biggest house I could ill afford in the nicest area. It was this, I later found out, that was the best move we could ever have made in our lives. If you have ten quid in the bank, you have enough for a bottle of wine. A hundred quid in the bank gives you enough for a drink, a meal and a night out. Many people with that amount feel they have "arrived" without realising how precarious their position is. I once read an article by a lady who described herself as a middle-class professional. Approaching her forties, she had read and heard the expression of being just two wage cheques away from sleeping on a park bench but dismissed it as a scenario that she would never be in. Wearing a pinstriped suit to work in a high paid job in the city, in a nice flat, with nice colleagues who drank and socialised every night, she was secure in her position. Her future was secure. Until she lost her job. Confident she could get another equally well-paid job quickly, she didn't worry. But she couldn't get a job. Soon her savings disappeared. Within six weeks, she was in arrears with her rent. Within two months, she was sleeping on a park bench. Her friends had disappeared. She had no money, nothing.

Hindsight is a wonderful thing. I have never thought I am cleverer than anyone else, far from it. But looking back, the one advantage I had was being self-employed and the fear from the moment I became self-employed. You realise how precarious your position is in life. Having kids focuses the mind with even more clarity. With my wife's backing, we set out to buy/pay for our house at the earliest opportunity. Having done that, we then set out to help our kids with their first car and then their weddings. Once that was out of the way, we focused on being able to retire at the earliest age possible and seek to enjoy the rest of our days in comfort, enjoying our lives. When we bought our motorhome, it opened up a world of freedom we grasped with both hands.

I hope you have read and enjoyed my book. When we bought our first motorhome, I realised we didn't have a clue. What do we carry on board? What cooking utensils, pots and pans, clothing, and accessories. It was all bewildering. Then there was, where do we go? Where can I camp up? What about wild camping? After all, we are totally self-contained. There were no books, only the advice of other motor homers we asked for. Other forums were cropping up. And even then, there was a mishmash of answers. How much does it cost to travel to Barmouth? To Dover? From Dover to the Riviera, from Calais to Alicante, it all sounded terrifying. But as Bet and I did it, we realised how straightforward it all was. Still is. France is twice the size of England, with less than half the people.

I wrote my first guide, a travel book, hoping it would help others in the same situation as us. It is called TOURING EUROPE ON A BUDGET (and a wing and a prayer) because that's exactly what it was. My second book followed, about some of the medieval castles and villages around Europe, France and the Pyrenees. Not forgetting the vineyards, of course. It is called HAPPY CAMPING AROUND EUROPE because that's what we do.

I'm not an author. I'm still the snot-nosed kid from Nechells with no future who made one for ourselves. I don't think we did too bad. If you can afford it, please buy one. I hope you enjoy them as much as we enjoyed doing them. Still do.

CAMPING TIPS

1. Always keep your motorhome well stocked with clothes for everyday use. I keep my wardrobe and cupboards stocked with various summer wear, shoes, socks, underpants, jigsaw games, etc. I have sewing kits, scissors, haircutters, tools, screwdrivers and super glue.

2. Likewise, regarding food, I keep all my cupboards full of dried foods, soups, sugar, coffee, tea, powdered milk, never fresh milk, saccharin, even Fray Bentos tinned pies, with a tin of veg they make a handy, cheap meal in minutes.

3. My camper is my home. I keep it stocked as I would my house. I keep my 80-litre water tank at least a quarter full, topping up as required. I carry two 13kg gas bottles in my container and another spare, especially for abroad. They last me six months.

4. Whilst my camper is my second home, certain rules and common sense must apply. I am quite frugal when it comes to cooking. A Fray Bentos pie will go in the oven and be served in its tin on a plate with a side of vegetables. When finished, the tin goes in the rubbish bag; the plate is wiped. If I fry an egg with bacon, I simply use a paper towel to wipe the nonstick frying pan. No wasting water. I usually eat out. The idea of cooking a three-course Sunday lunch seems ridiculous in a motorhome.

5. If using water, be even more frugal. For a shower, it's wet hair, turn off, put on shampoo, wash off and turn off. In the sink, I use bottled water to clean my teeth. Wash,

brush, and rinse. Mostly outside. 80 litres of water might sound like a lot, but it disappears mighty fast. I rarely use the shower. Why do you have to clean yourself so often if you are not dirty? If I'm near a stream, I wash in that. A quick dip in the sea and I'm as right as rain after a swim. Yes, ok, it's your home, but common sense prevails over the way utilities are going up. Few of us will afford a bath soon anyway.

6. If you require water, most garages should be able to help. If not, try the nearest cemetery. In the country, try the local farmer. My go-to place by the sea is the nearest marina. All marinas have taps.

7. Most of the above applies to me alone, but when my wife was with me, we still more or less kept the same rules, though we cooked outside more. My wife had priority over the toilet and water, and every few days, we would find a site to top up, refresh and empty waste. I never use the toilet to pee, preferring to use a plastic container emptying it in a suitable discreet place.

8. I try not to use sites at all, especially in England. £30 just to park up, empty your waste and use the electricity whilst on a patch of wet grass seems, well, over the top to me. They may as well put up signs saying campers are not welcome in England. I have solar panels, as well as a shower, fridge, cooker, and television. I am completely self-contained and sufficient.

9. Finally, treat your outings or expeditions as an adventure, whether it be a 2 or 3-day break around England or something longer, like a European tour where the attitude to motorhomes is quite different. In France, there are Aires in abundance. I have swum in the sea mere feet from my motorhome. In the Tarn Gorge also, I swam in the river only feet away. On motorways, I always park as close to the restaurants or services as possible overnight. In Italy, parked in a car park by the beach, I was treated to the delightful sight of wild boar coming out of the forest

to be fed by the locals. In the mountains, we saw wild boar and wild bears. You won't get that on a campsite.

I am sure other people have even better and even more ideas for savings. Happy camping. The next stop is the Scottish 500 and the highlands.

THE END